He has Anointed Me

Pat Collins C.M.

First edition published in 2005 by
New Life Publishing, 15 Barking Close
Luton, Beds. LU4 9HG
orders@goodnewsbooks.net

British Library Cataloguing in Publication Data
A catalogue record for this book is
available from the British Library

Bible references taken from the
N.I.V. and N.R.S.V. versions of the Bible

ISBN 1 903623 18 9

Typesetting by New Life Publishing.
Printed in the UK by Print Solutions,
Wallington, Surrey.

Acknowledgment

To all at GoodNews magazine
for their support and encouragement

The cover design for this book depicts people coming to the Lord with their burdens and shows how His anointing brings freedom and empowers them for service. It is from a painting by Yvonne Bell, commissioned for the Celebrate Conference 2004.

Yvonne is a Christian artist and designer.
Her work can be seen on her web site:
www.vestments.co.uk

Contents

Foreword i
Introduction iii

1   Does the Catholic Church Approve
     of Charismatic Renewal? 1
2   Was St Patrick a Charismatic? 7
3   Misery and Mercy 12
4   The Divine Indwelling 18
5   Tongues and Contemplation 24
6   Thanking God in all Circumstances 29
7   Words of Knowledge 36
8   The Charism of Faith 42
9   The Working of Miracles 48
10   The Ministry of Deliverance 53
11   The Exorcism of Mother Teresa 65
12   The Gift of Prophecy 75
13   Is Prophecy about Catastrophe or Hope? 84
14   Witnesses to the Supernatural 103
15   Charismatics and Christian Maturity 109
16   Charisms and the New Evangelisation 115
17   Charisms and Ecumenism 123
18   Apostasy and Hope 128
19   Charismatics and Contemporary Ethics 135
20   Overcoming Feelings of Injustice and Hurt 140
21   The New Age Movement Evaluated 154
22   Reading Scripture and Religious Experience 160
23   The Gift of Generosity 168
24   An Examen of Consciousness 177
25   A Charismatic Check-up 183

Foreword

It gives me great pleasure to write the foreword to this book by Fr. Pat Collins on the Charismatic Renewal, which deals with many of the basic questions about the charisms and their relevance to everyday life.

I knew Fr. Pat long before I ever met him personally, as back in the 1980's our prayer group used to listen every week to a tape series he had developed with Agape Tapes of short teachings on the basics of Charismatic Renewal. These ten minute talks were short, sound and very helpful to our group when we didn't know very much about all these things.

In more recent years Fr. Pat has become a friend and a much valued and stimulating presence on the Goodnews editorial committee, as well as being one of our most popular contributing writers. This is because he has that rare ability among academics to be able to communicate spiritual truths in an accessible and interesting way for the non-specialist. I always look forward to what he writes as I know I will learn something new and be challenged and gain some fascinating new insight or perspective on things.

Fr. Pat reads a lot and travels a lot and he is interested in everything. This wide range of interests is apparent in his writing and he draws together nuggets from many disciplines and these help to inform his work. They also give him an ability to look at Charismatic Renewal from the outside as well as from the inside and to develop a language that can help explain Charismatic Renewal to others. The Renewal certainly needs apologists like him and I'm sure those who have questions about the Charismatic Renewal will find some useful answers among these pages.

Kristina Cooper
Editor, GoodNews Magazine

Introduction

I thank God that I was baptised in the Holy Spirit on the 4th of February 1974. It led to a spiritual awakening in my Christian life. By the grace of God I was enabled to have a new and vivid awareness of the presence, love and activity of God working in and through me. Sometimes it was expressed in charismatic ways. Thankfully, over the years I have received subsequent in-fillings of the Spirit which have tended to deepen and strengthen that initial blessing.

I have often reflected in a prayerful way on the nature and implications of new life in the Spirit, both for myself and others. Then I have tried to share my insights in homilies, talks and books. Over the years, I have also written numerous articles on charismatic subjects. They have been published in a number of magazines such as New Creation in Ireland, Good News in Britain, and Ruah in Italy. Recently, I decided to collect a number of them in book form. My hope is that they will not only provide those who read them with interesting information about many aspects of charismatic spirituality, but that they will also lead to prayer and meditation of a fruitful kind.

Sometimes, in the past, when I have thought about possible titles for books I had written, I have had to agonise for months considering one possibility after another. However, as soon as I thought about this book, it immediately occurred to me that it should be entitled, *He Has Anointed Me*. There are two main reasons for this. Firstly, Jesus became the Christ when he was anointed by the Holy Spirit during his baptism in the Jordan so that he might bring the Good News to the poor (Cf. Luke 4: 18). As St Peter was to testify many years later: 'You have heard how God anointed Jesus of Nazareth with the Holy Spirit and power' Acts 10: 38. Secondly, when we Christians are baptised in the Holy Spirit we share in Christ's anointing. As scripture says: 'You have an anointing from the Holy One, and all of you know the truth..... the anointing you received from him remains in you, and you do not need anyone to teach you. But as his anointing teaches you about all things and as that anointing is real, not counterfeit-- just as it has taught you, remain in him.' 1 John 2: 20; 2: 27.

The Greek word for anointing in this text is *chrisma* which refers to a blessing or unction with oil as the outward sign of an inner blessing of the Holy Spirit. I have often thought that it was unfortunate that our Movement was referred to as 'charismatic,' (which focuses attention on the gifts of the Spirit) rather than 'chrismatic' (which focuses on the anointing of the Spirit). It is my hope that the disparate chapters in

this book will not only help Charismatics to have a
better understanding of the graces they have already
received or still hope to receive, but will also help
non-Charismatics to have a better insight into this
form of influential spirituality.

Chapter One

Does the Catholic Church Approve of Charismatic Renewal?

Over they years I, like many other members of the Charismatic Renewal, have encountered resistance to the movement. I think that one possible cause is an unacknowledged fear of anything new that might require people to change, not only their relationship with God, but also the way in which they live their lives. Sometimes the critics of the Charismatic Renewal say such things as, 'it is too emotional', 'it is too pious and neglects social justice issues', or 'Charismatic Renewal has its origins in the Protestant Churches, and is neither genuinely Catholic nor in accord with the teachings of the Church'. In this short chapter I want to indicate how the latter criticism is not correct.

He Has Anointed Me

Attitude of the Popes

In 1961 Pope John XXIII prayed, 'Divine Spirit, renew your wonders in our time, as though for a new Pentecost.' In the years following the Second Vatican Council, many renewal movements came into being one of which was the Charismatic Renewal. Pope Paul VI often spoke about it. For example, on Pentecost Monday 1976, the first 'charismatic mass' was celebrated in St Peter's. At the end of the Eucharist he said: 'How then could this 'spiritual renewal' not be a 'chance' for the church and the world?.... It ought to rejuvenate the world, give it back a spirituality, a soul, a religious thought, it ought to reopen its closed lips to prayer and open its mouth to song, to joy, to hymns, and to witnessing. It will be fortuitous for our times, for our brothers and sisters, that there should be a generation of young people, who shout out to the world the greatness of the God of Pentecost.'

In 1978, Edward O' Connor published *Pope Paul and The Spirit*. It included an excellent overview of Pope Paul's teaching on the Holy Spirit which was followed by transcripts of his many addresses on the subject. Amongst other things, Pope Paul said in par. 75 of his influential encyclical *On Evangelisation in the Modern World*: 'We are living in a privileged moment of the Spirit in the Church. People everywhere are trying to know him better as he is revealed in scripture. They are happy to place themselves under his inspiration. They gather around him; they want to be guided by him. But while the Spirit of God has a pre-eminent place in the entire life of the Church, he is active above all in the mission of evangelisation.'

Speaking to a Charismatic gathering in 1981, Pope John Paul II said: 'Pope Paul described the movement for renewal in the Spirit as a chance for the Church and for the world, and the six years since have borne out the hope that inspired his vision. The Church has seen the fruits of your devotion to prayer in a deepened commitment to holiness of life and love for the word of God . . . May the work of love already begun in you be brought to successful completion!' In 1998 the Pontiff said: 'the Catholic Charismatic movement is one of the many fruits of Vatican Council II which stimulated an extraordinary flourishing of groups and movements especially sensitive to the Holy Spirit.'

Attitude of the Bishops

Some time ago, Cardinal Ratzinger, Prefect of the Sacred Congregation for the Doctrine of Faith, echoed the sentiments of Pope John Paul II when he said: 'What is hopeful at the level of the universal Church – and what is happening right in the heart of the crisis of the Church in the Western world – is the rise of new movements which nobody had planned and which nobody has called into being, but which have sprung spontaneously from the inner vitality of the faith itself. What is manifested in them – albeit in a subdued way – is something like a Pentecostal season in the Church. I am thinking, say, of the Charismatic Movement, of the Cursillos.' He went on to say that he had noted the effectiveness of the Charismatic Movement in Munich. Among other things it had provided good quality

3

vocations to the priesthood.

Toward the end of the last century, fifty different Catholic renewal movements and communities, including the Charismatics, gathered in Rome, on the Vigil of Pentecost 1998. The Vatican estimated that more than half a million people attended the celebration. In its June edition, the magazine entitled, *Inside the Vatican* stated in its editorial: 'what happened in May in Rome was so important we believe that future historians of the Church will have to distinguish between 'before' and 'after' Pentecost 1998.' Apparently, the Pope saw the renewal movements as a hopeful sign of an impending springtime in the Church. Subsequently, he said: 'The abundant tears of humanity during the 20th century open up the hope of a new spring... I am convinced that the year 2000 will be an incomparable occasion to make the mystery of faith and the re-flourishing of Christianity present in a society filled with anguish and asphyxia by secularism.'

Many episcopal conferences and individual bishops have also approved of the Charismatic Renewal and its distinctive spirituality. For example in 1997, the United States Conference of Bishops wrote a document of the Charismatic Renewal entitled, *Grace for A New Springtime*. Among other things they said: 'The Catholic Charismatic Renewal is, as Pope John Paul II said in 1979, a sign of the Holy Spirit's action.... and a very important component of the total renewal of the Church... The impact of the Charismatic Renewal on

4

the broader church has been significant. The Renewal has nourished the call of all to holiness as a gift from the Spirit and helped the Church come to a greater awareness and expectancy of the Holy Spirit and the charismatic gifts of the Spirit. The Charismatic Renewal has led the people of God in a revival of the ministry of healing, encouraging them - laity and clergy alike – to pray for the sick with expectancy.' The document goes on to say: 'Charismatic empowerment in community has supplied the Church in this country and throughout the world with a host of committed and effective evangelists bringing the gospel to persons and places otherwise without hope of hearing the good news.'

In 1993, the Irish bishops published *New Life in the Spirit: Pastoral Guidance on the Charismatic Renewal.* On page six the bishops say that they: 'have seen many fruits of the Charismatic Renewal during the past twenty years. Thousands have found deeper commitment to Christ, a deep love for the Holy Scriptures, an openness to the gifts of the Holy Spirit, profound gifts of prayer, greater understanding of the Eucharist and of the Church, a fruitful love of their brothers and sisters. Charismatic communities have grown up which support their members' commitment and are of service to the local Church.'

Conclusion

While the local and universal Church has given approval to the renewal movements it has warned it, as it would any similar movement, against dangers and excesses. For instance, in his encyclical on Catechesis, John Paul II said in par. 72: 'Renewal in the Spirit will be authentic and will have real fruitfulness in the Church, not so much according as it gives rise to extraordinary charisms, but according as it leads the greatest possible number of the faithful, as they travel their daily paths, to make a humble, patient and persevering effort to know the mystery of Christ better and better, and to bear witness to it.' Amen to that!

Chapter 2

Was St Patrick a Charismatic?

Before deciding whether St Patrick was a Charismatic or not, it is necessary to state what criteria could be used in making a judgement. I will mention three. Firstly, the person needs to experience a spiritual awakening as a result of an in-filling by the Holy Spirit. In a pastoral entitled, *Life in the Spirit*, the Irish bishops described this grace as follows: 'The outpouring of the Holy Spirit is a conversion gift through which one receives a new and significant commitment to the Lordship of Jesus and openness to the power and gifts of the Holy Spirit.' The American bishops provided a more comprehensive definition when they said in 1997 in a document entitled *Grace for a New Springtime*, 'As experienced in the Catholic Charismatic Renewal, baptism in the Spirit makes Jesus Christ known and loved as Lord and Saviour, establishes or re-establishes an immediacy of relationship with all those persons of the Trinity, and through inner transformation affects the whole of the Christian life. There is new life and a new conscious awareness of God's power and presence.' Secondly, a Charismatic is a person who has received either ordinary gifts, such as alms giving and administration, or more extraordinary gifts of the Spirit, such as those mentioned in 1 Corinthians 12: 8-10. Thirdly, like Jesus, a true Charismatic desires to be led and guided by the Spirit in all the circumstances of his or her life (cf. Gal 5: 18). Judged by these three standards, it seems clear from Patrick's Confessions that Ireland's national saint was a charismatic.

Baptism in the Spirit

Evidently Patrick was not gospel greedy as a teenager in Roman Britain. He says: 'I did not believe in the living God from my childhood.' However, when he was brought to Ireland as a captive, he experienced a crisis. In the midst of his afflictions he began to have a heartfelt desire for a revelation of God. Speaking about his subsequent baptism in the Spirit he said: 'I cannot hide the gift of God which he gave me in the land of my captivity. There I sought him and there I found him. The Lord made me aware of my unbelief that I might at last advert to my sins and turn wholeheartedly to the Lord my God.' As a result of his conversion and religious awakening, Patrick says: 'More and more my faith grew stronger and my zeal so intense that in the course of a single day I would say as many as a hundred prayers, and almost as many as night.'

Charismatic Activity

As one reads the *Confessions* of St Patrick one is reminded of the life of Paul as recounted in the Acts of the Apostles. They are full of charismatic references.

At one point, Patrick refers to the prophecy of Joel which was quoted by St Peter on Pentecost Sunday. It says: 'Your young men shall see visions, and your old men shall dream dreams' Acts 2:17. Patrick himself recounts a number of the religious dreams and visions he experienced. He escaped from Ireland as a result of a revelatory dream and returned to the country as a result of another.

He also had the gift of expectant faith (cf. 1 Corinthians 12:9). On one occasion he told his captors when they were starving in war ravaged Britain: 'Turn sincerely with your whole heart to the Lord my God, because nothing is impossible to him.' A little later he says: 'Suddenly a herd of pigs appeared on the road before our eyes, they killed many of them.'

Patrick also witnesses to the fact that he was able to intercede in the Spirit. He adverts to the well known passage on this subject in Romans 8: 23-27 which says: 'I saw a praying person in me…. All this time I was puzzled as I wondered greatly who could possibly be praying in me. He spoke however at the end of the prayer, saying that he was the Spirit.'

There is even reason to believe that he may have

prayed in tongues (cf. Mark 16:17; 1 Corinthians 12:10). In one place he quotes Romans 8: 26: 'The Spirit expresses our plea with great emotion in a way that cannot be put into words.' This verse probably refers to intercession in non conceptual language or sounds. In another place in the *Confessions*, he says that when he was praying fervently he heard words, 'but could not understand them.' Once again, he infers that he may have been praying in tongues.

It is clear from other passages that he had received infused knowledge about future events (cf. 1 Corinthians 12: 8). For example, he says that: 'On my first night among my captors I received a divine message which said; 'you will be with them for two months.' That is just what happened.' Later he adds: 'God, who knows all things in advance, is my witness that he used to forewarn me often by a divine message.' In another place he says: 'I foretold events and still foretell them in order to strengthen and consolidate your faith.'

Lastly, Patrick had the gift of being an apostle (cf. Ephesians 4:11), a remarkable ability to evangelise effectively. 'Through me,' he testifies, 'many people were born again in God and afterwards confirmed.'

Conclusion

In the *Confessions*, Patrick often speaks about his life in the Spirit e.g. 'I am tied by the Spirit...I am convinced that God keeps me from all evil because his Spirit lives in me and works in me to this very day.' Like our Lord he was led by the Spirit. He received guidance, as we have seen, in different forms such as dreams, visions, and inspired messages. For instance, at one point during his mission in Ireland, Patrick desired to visit Britain in order to see his relatives. He says: 'God knows I greatly desired it, but I am bound by the Spirit, who protests to me that if I do this he will pronounce me guilty.' Speaking about his mission to the Irish he said: 'It was not really I who began it but Christ the Lord who told me to come here and stay with them for the rest of my life.' Later in the *Confessions* he says: 'From the time in my early manhood when I came to know him, the love of God and reverence for him have grown in me, and up to now, by the favour of God, I have kept the faith.' Clearly, the great apostle of Ireland was filled, gifted, and guided by the Holy Spirit.

Chapter 3

Misery and Mercy

Ever since I was a boy I have asked myself the question, how can we reconcile the justice and the mercy of God? On the one hand, we say that God rewards the good and punishes the wicked. For example in Matthew 6: 12, Jesus says: 'The Son of Man is going to come in the glory of his Father with his angels, and, when he does, he will reward each one according to his behaviour.' Again St Paul says: 'by your hard and impenitent heart you are storing up wrath for yourself on the day of wrath, when God's righteous judgment will be revealed. For he will repay according to each one's deeds' Romans 2: 5-6. On the other hand, we say that God overlooks our sins and grants unconditional and unrestricted mercy to those who trust in him. Jesus said, 'You judge according to the flesh, but I judge no one.... for I did not come to judge the world but to save the world' John 8: 15; John 12: 47. St Paul says: 'There is therefore now no condemnation for those who are in Christ Jesus' Romans 8: 1. In seeking an answer to this dilemma I have been greatly helped by the spirituality of St Therese of Lisieux.

St Therese on the Justice and Mercy of God

In the 19th century, the French Carmelites saw themselves as victims of divine justice, women who took upon themselves the punishments that should rightfully have been meted out to great sinners. Therese couldn't accept this emphasis. When she was fifteen years of age she had been graced with a vivid experience of the length and breadth, the height and depth of God's incomprehensible love for her.

Some years later, a companion of Therese was nearing death. Sr. Febronie was her name. She was so focused on divine justice that she was terrified of having to face God's judgement and his punishments. Therese, reminded the elderly nun that she had tried to live a good life. If perchance, she had fallen short in any way, all she had to do was to trust in God's great mercy. Therese said: 'Our Lord is very justice; if he doesn't judge our good actions, he will not judge our bad ones either. For those who offer themselves to love, I don't think there will be a judgement at all.' Apparently, Sr. Ferbronie wasn't convinced. Eventually Therese said to her, 'Sister, if you want divine justice, you will get divine justice. The soul gets exactly what it expects from God.' In other words you have to choose the kind of God you believe in, a fearful God of justice, or a reassuring God of mercy.

Fr. P. Marie-Eugene has suggested that Therese's understanding of God's mercy led her to cultivate the 'art of failure.' She would intend to do some good act but would sometimes fail to do so, for one reason or another. Apparently, she would then say: 'If I had been faithful I would have received the reward of merit by appealing to God's justice. I was unfaithful, I am humiliated, I am going to receive the reward of my poverty and humiliation by appealing to God's mercy.' She believed that she would be rewarded in times of humiliating failure by God's merciful love. What a remarkable insight into the loving kindness of the heart of our God. I suspect that Therese's failures were small compared to our own. Nevertheless, the principle she enunciates remains the same. Indeed, it could be argued that the greater and the more humiliating the failure the greater the graces that are lavished upon the grieving heart. God does not react in accordance with what we deserve but in accordance with the Divine nature which loves us unconditionally.

As a result of all these insights Therese was able to offer herself to Divine love, rather than Divine justice in 1895. Sometime afterwards she said: 'After earth's exile, I hope to go and enjoy you in the fatherland, but I do not to lay up merits for heaven. I want to work for your love alone.... In the evening of this life, I shall appear before you with empty hands, for I do not ask you Lord, to count my works. All our justice is blemished in your eyes. I wish, then, to be clothed in your own justice and to receive from your love the eternal possession of yourself.' It would seem that for Therese, God's justice was subsumed into the divine mercy, so that they became virtually synonymous.

The Justice and Mercy of God in Scripture

I find that the teaching of Therese on the mercy of God is not only reassuring, it is firmly rooted in scripture as the story about the woman caught in adultery in John 8: 1-11 attests. It was not in the original version of the gospel. However, this episode, reminiscent of others recounted in the Synoptics, was accepted as inspired by the Church. It was inserted into the text in the third century.

The Pharisees are out to trap Jesus. The woman has been caught in the act of adultery. In terms of strict justice, the situation was clear. She was guilty of the offence, and Deuteronomy 22: 23-24 stipulated that, as a married woman, she should be stoned to death. However, Roman law did not allow the Jews to execute a person for religious reasons. So they asked Jesus, what they should do. If he said, 'Stone her in accordance with the law,' he would have been disobeying civil law and denying his own teachings on divine mercy (cf. John 3: 17; 12: 47). If, on the other hand, he said: 'Don't stone her,' he would have been contradicting precepts of scripture.

In the event, with wisdom, characteristic of Solomon of old, Jesus changed the whole focus of the debate by saying: 'Let him who is without sin among you be the first to throw a stone at her.' In other words, if anyone present is innocent of sin, if he has never lusted after a woman in his heart (cf. Matthew 5: 27ff.) let him be the first to dispense justice. One by one, beginning with the eldest, all the men slinked away because all of them had to acknowledge their own guilty secrets. Jesus and the woman were left facing one another. As St Augustine observed, she was the personification of *miseria* i.e. misery, while he was the personification of *misercordia* i.e. mercy.

Measured against his own criterion of sinlessness, Jesus had a right to stone the woman. But he didn't exercise that right. In John 8:10 we are told that he asked: 'Has no one condemned you? She said, 'No one Lord.' And Jesus said, 'Neither do I condemn you; go and do not sin again.' What wonderful, liberating words. Later on, they were to find an echo in Romans 8: 1: 'There is now no condemnation for those who are in Christ Jesus.' In other words, they are declared not guilty and acquitted, and free from punishment. How should we respond to this Good News? In Luke 6: 36-37 Jesus says that we should: 'Be merciful, just as your Father is merciful.' Do not judge, and you will not be judged. Do not condemn, and you will not be condemned. Forgive, and you will be forgiven.'

Conclusion

Before his death, Pope Paul VI told Fr. John McGee, now bishop of Cloyne, how he had been deeply influenced by the two words, misery and mercy, in

St Augustine's commentary on John 8: 1-8. 'Always, in all of us,' he said, 'there is a tension between my misery and God's mercy. The whole spiritual life of all of us lies between these two poles. If I open myself to the action of God and the Holy Spirit and let them do with me what they will, then my tension becomes joyous and I feel within myself a greater desire to come to him and receive his mercy; more than ever I recognise the need to be forgiven, to receive the gift of mercy. Then I feel the need to say thanks, and so my whole life becomes a thanksgiving, a Eucharist to God because he has saved me, redeemed me, drawn me to himself in love. It is not anything I have done in my life that saves me, but God's mercy.'

Recently I came across a passage from the writings of St Bernard, one which echoed the point just made. 'The whole of the spiritual life', he stated, 'turns on these two things: we are troubled when we contemplate ourselves and our sorrow brings salvation; when we contemplate God we are restored, so that we receive consolation from the joy of the Holy Spirit. From the contemplation of ourselves (i.e. misery) we gain fear and humility; from the contemplation of God (i.e. mercy) hope and love.'

Chapter 4

The Divine Indwelling

A number of years ago some Travellers in North Dublin asked me to say an inaugural mass in a hut they had built on their halting site. The following day I returned to the site and visited the families who were living there. When I knocked on one caravan door, it was opened by a good looking young woman with blonde hair. She gave me a warm welcome, invited me in, and said, 'I'm glad you called, father, because there is something I want to tell you.' When I asked her what it was, she replied: 'I was at the mass last night. When you gave out holy communion you said that we should close our eyes and imagine that Jesus was standing in front of us looking at us with eyes full of love and humility.' 'Yes, I can remember saying that,' I responded. 'Well, father,' said the travelling woman, 'I did see Jesus standing in front of me. He was as real to me as you are at the moment.' 'So you saw Jesus, after receiving holy communion,' I said, 'that must have been deeply moving.' 'It was, father, but that wasn't all. Jesus walked into me.' 'What do you mean?' I asked. 'Father, Jesus walked through my skin into my body. I knew he was living inside me.' 'That is wonderful,' I whispered, 'what did you feel when you knew that Jesus was living within you?' The young woman paused; then she replied, 'Joyful: I never felt so happy in all my life. In fact, I still feel the same happiness today.' I had only to look at her radiant face to know that what she said was true.

Surely, this young Traveller had an experiential awareness of the meaning of the following texts: 'Remain in me,' said Jesus, 'and I will remain in you' John 15: 4; 'the life I live now is not my own; Christ is living in me' Galatians 2: 20 and we are 'sharers of the divine nature' 2 Peter 1: 4.

Relationship and Identity

In spirituality as in psychology, inwardness and relatedness are interconnected. Paradoxically, the more I relate to others, the more I discover and relate to my own deepest self. Carl Jung, one of the most introspective of psychologists stated: 'One is always in the dark about one's personality. One needs others to get to know oneself.' If any of us reflect on our friendships we become aware of the fact that we grow in self-awareness through our struggle to grow in intimacy. It confronts us with the limits of such things as our trust, generosity, patience and our ability to receive.

As I contemplate God the Father, in and through his Son, I get to know my own divine potential, my Christ-self. Pope John Paul II adverted to this principle in paragraph eight of his encyclical, *Veritatis Splendor:* 'the man who wishes to understand himself should…. draw near to Christ. He must, so to speak, enter him with all his own self, …. If this profound process takes place within him, he then bears fruit not only of adoration of God but also of deeper wonder at himself.'

In another place the Holy Father said: 'God is present in the intimacy of man's being, in his mind, conscience and heart; an ontological and psychological reality.' When the Pope talks about the divine indwelling as an ontological reality, he means that, in virtue of my baptism, it is a certain fact, whether I'm consciously aware of it, or not. It becomes a psychological reality as a result of a spiritual awakening such as baptism in the Spirit. When I'm filled with the Spirit, I have the felt sense, as Thomas Merton expressed it, that: 'My deepest realisation of who I am is – I am one loved by Christ….The depths of my identity is in the centre of my being where I am loved by God.'

Christ's Biography My Potential Autobiography

Should I imitate Christ? or is his biography my potential autobiography? On one occasion Carl Jung asked: 'Are we to understand the imitation of Christ in the sense that we should copy his life, or in the deeper sense that we are to live our own proper lives as he lived his in its individual uniqueness?' Surely the latter understanding is the more correct one. Par 521 of the *Catechism of the Catholic Church* describes the profound effects of the divine indwelling which began with the sacraments of initiation: 'Christ enables us to live in him all that he himself lived, and he lives it in us.'

In his *The Life and Kingdom of Jesus in Christian Souls*, St John Eudes (1601-1688), drew out an important implication of this spiritual truth. He began by quoting a well known Pauline text: 'I make up what is lacking in the sufferings of Jesus Christ for the sake of his body the Church' Colossians 1: 24. He then went on to observe that what Paul says about our sufferings can be extended to all our other actions as well. He said that any true Christian, who is united to Christ by his grace, continues and fulfils, through all the actions that he carries out in the spirit of Christ, the actions that Jesus Christ performed during his brief life on earth. So ....

• When a Christian prays, he continues and fulfils the prayer that Jesus Christ offered on earth.

• Whenever she works, she continues and fulfils the laborious efforts of Jesus Christ.

• Whenever he relates to his neighbour in a spirit of unconditional love, then he continues and fulfils the relational life of Jesus Christ.

• Whenever she eats or rests in a Christian manner, she continues and fulfils the subjection that Jesus Christ wished to have to these necessities.

The same can be said of any other action that is carried out in a Christian manner.

It is interesting to note however, that John Eudes says nothing about exercising the charisms Jesus exercised, such as healing, exorcism and miracle working. St Vincent de Paul, a contemporary of Eudes, made the same omission. He said on one occasion, 'When our Lord imprints his mark on us and gives us, so to say, the sap of his spirit and grace we, *being united to him as the branches are united to the vine, will do what he did when he was on earth* (my italics), I mean to say, we will perform divine actions and beget, like St Paul, beings filled with this spirit, children to our Lord.' Both saints were writing at a time when the charisms were largely inactive. But surely the logic of their positions indicated that if Christians could do what Jesus did, it implied the possibility of deeds of power. Indeed, Jesus promised as much when he said: 'Amen, Amen, I say to you, whoever believes in me will do the works I do, and will do greater ones than these, because I am going to my Father. And whatever you ask in my name, I will do, so that the Father may be glorified in the Son. If you ask anything in my name, I will do it' John 14:12.

A Prayer

I must confess that, over the last year or two, in particular, this awareness has become a central tenet of my personal spirituality. When I'm about to embark on different tasks such as writing, preaching, teaching, praying for others; struggling to love, to be patient, to be generous, to resist temptation etc., I often run into the buffers of my own natural weakness and limitations. But then I say to Jesus:

'Lord, the good I wish to do, I cannot do, but you are living out the mysteries of your life in me. Enable me by the Spirit that animated your life of loving service, to continue and fulfil that same loving service in my own life. Give me the ability to do this task (state what it is…..), and I thank you that you are achieving even more than I can ask, or imagine through the power of your Spirit, even now, at work within me.'

I have found that when I affirm the divine indwelling, in this way, I have the conviction, not only that my efforts are being blessed, but that they will bear lasting fruit.

Chapter 5

Tongues and Contemplation

Be advised, there is no simple way to write about this subject. However, I will try to make it as clear and straight forward as possible. The word 'contemplation' is often misunderstood. It is derived from Latin, and literally means 'to look at, to pay sustained attention.' We can contemplate anything, either the bible of the created world, or the Bible of sacred scripture when we focus our minds upon them in a single-minded, undistracted way. As we do so, God's mysterious presence can be, partially and indirectly, revealed to us.

Spiritual writers have always maintained that there are two interrelated forms of contemplation. The first, known as 'the positive way' stresses the knowability of God, albeit in an incomplete and veiled way, in the form of ideas and images. The second, known as 'the negative way' stresses the un-knowability of God whose incomprehensible mystery, ultimately, lies beyond the grasp of the mind and imagination.

Prayer Without Ideas or Images

Down the centuries there have been many writers who have advocated methods which would help people to engage in the second form of contemplative prayer. For example, in the 4th century, John Cassian said that those who wished to pray without ceasing in a contemplative manner should use a mantra. He suggested that they should repeat the verse, 'O Lord come to my assistance, O Lord make haste to help me' (Psalm 70: 1), in the belief that it summed up the spirituality of the entire bible. He stressed that those who used this formula shouldn't dwell on its meaning. In the Middle Ages, the anonymous English author of *The Cloud of Unknowing*, encouraged people to repeat a single word, such as 'God' or 'Love' rather than a religious phrase. In the 19th century the unknown author of *The Way of the Pilgrim* discovered that he could pray unceasingly, in a contemplative way, by repeating the Jesus Prayer, 'Lord Jesus Christ, have mercy on me a sinner.' In the 20th century, a number of spiritual guides, such as John Main and Basil Pennington have advocated the use of mantras in what is known as Centering Prayer.

Phyllis Campbell expressed one of the central aims of these forms of prayer when she wrote: 'Serene Light, shining in the ground of my being, draw me to

Yourself. Draw me past the snares of the senses, out of the mazes of the mind; free me from symbols, from words, that I may discover the Signified, the Word unspoken, in the darkness which veils the ground of my being. '

Tongues and Mantras Contrasted

When I read what writers like Cassian had to say about the negative way of contemplating the Lord, it struck me that many of those who pray in tongues are familiar with this kind of prayer. St. Paul wrote in 1 Corinthians 14: 2;14 that those who pray in a tongue: 'do not speak to other people but to God; for nobody understands them, since they are speaking mysteries in the Spirit... if I pray in a tongue my spirit prays but my mind is unproductive.' In Romans 8: 27 he added: 'and God who searches the heart, knows what is the mind of the Spirit, because the Spirit prays.... according to the will of God.'

It has also occurred to me that when charismatic activity faded during the first three centuries, people like Cassian and the others, had to find an alternative. So they resorted to the repetitive use of selected phrases and words, in order to pray in an imageless, conceptless way. But with the contemporary revival of the charism of praying and singing in tongues, a growing number of people have rediscovered a truly scriptural way of enabling their spirits to commune with God without the aid of mind or imagination.

Cassian stated that by using a mantra, people are

prepared to read the scriptures with spiritual insight. Like a surgeon's scalpel, their minds are enabled to cut to the most intimate meaning of God's word. Those who use the gift of praying in tongues have a similar experience. The charism ploughs the soil of their hearts, making them ready to receive the seed of God's revelatory word and the refreshing waters of the Spirit. One is reminded in this connection of the two kinds of prophetic experience in the Old Testament, ecstatic and classical. The earlier Old Testament prophets experienced an ecstasy in the divine presence without any apparent conceptual or verbal content (cf. 1 Samuel 19: 20-21). Some time later, the classical prophets, such as Elijah, Ezekiel, Jeremiah and Isaiah, expressed in words what had first been revealed to them in a non-conceptual, ecstatic way. As scripture scholar, George Montague has observed, 'In Old Testament prophecy the pendulum swings between, the ecstatic, non-rational, pre-conceptual element and the intelligible, rational, spoken word. But in either case prophecy is essentially a gift of inspiration.'

Having prayed in tongues, divine inspirations can come to contemporary Christians in ordinary and extra-ordinary ways such as, inspiring words of scripture (cf. Hebrews 4: 12-13), prophetic messages (Cf: I Corinthians 14: 24-25), visions (cf. Joel 3: 1) religious dreams (Cf: Job 33: 1;5) words of knowledge (Cf: I Corinthians 12: 8), Spirit prompted intuitions (cf. Galatians 5: 16) etc. Anyone who prays in tongues will find that whatever inspiration he or she receives can be expressed by praying, firstly, with rational understanding, and secondly, in a non-conceptual, imageless way by means of tongues. As a result, in charismatic prayer there is a reciprocal relationship between non-conceptual imageless prayer and conceptual and imaginative prayer.

Conclusion

Having stated that he prayed in tongues more than anyone (1 Corinthians 14: 18), St Paul said that he would like everyone to exercise this ability (1 Corinthians 14: 5). Those who regularly use this gift know that it can take a number of forms, such as heartfelt intercession, loud and enthusiastic praise, and quiet, reverential worship. However, it is important that those in the Charismatic Movement should also appreciate the fact that praying and singing in tongues can lead those who are granted a special touch of the Holy Spirit, into one of the deeper forms of contemplative prayer. So earnestly desire the spiritual gifts (cf. 1 Corinthians 14: 1.), especially the charism of tongues which leads the loving will, if not the mind and imagination, into the mysterious presence of the One who lives in light inaccessible.

Chapter 6

Thanking God in All Circumstances

In Tobit 12: 6; 22, the messenger Raphael says to Tobit and his son Tobias: 'Praise God and give thanks to him; exalt him and give thanks to him in the presence of all the living for what he has done for you. It is good to acknowledge God and to exalt his name, worthily declaring the works of God. Do not be slow to give him thanks ......they stood up .....and confessed the great and wonderful works of God.' We can thank God for an endless list of blessings, such as salvation, health, special abilities, education, financial security etc.

Reading St Paul, it is evident that he saw thankful appreciation as an act of fundamental religious importance. By contemplating the existence and beauty of the created world, a rational human being could perceive the existence and character of its Maker. As 2 Maccabees 7: 28 says: 'look at the heaven and the earth and see everything that is in them, and recognise that God did not make them out of things that existed. Thus also mankind comes into being.' Paul echoed that sentiment when he wrote: 'For since the creation of the world, God's invisible qualities - his eternal power and divine nature - have been clearly seen, being understood from what has been made.'

Then Paul goes on to make an all important observation about unbelievers, 'For although they knew God, they neither glorified him as God nor gave thanks to him' Romans 1: 21. In other words, in Paul's mind lack of appreciation of the gifts of God is indicative of a culpable lack of reverence for the God of the gifts. For him, therefore, ingratitude and unbelief are virtually synonymous. Not only that, irreligion has dire consequences from a moral and social point of view. Paul echoes an observation of Judges 17: 6: 'In those days Israel had no king; everyone did as he saw fit.' Instead of honouring God, unbelievers idolise created things and either re-write or ignore the commandments to suit themselves: 'Because of this,' he says, 'God gave them over to shameful lusts' Romans 1: 26-31. Surely, Paul's indictment continues to have relevance in our secular culture where lack of grateful reverence of a religious kind is evident in moral permissiveness and social fragmentation.

Thanksgiving Always and for Everything

In marked contrast, St Paul not only thanks God

repeatedly himself, he says to people of faith: 'pray continually; give thanks in all circumstances, for this is God's will for you in Christ Jesus,' 1 Thessalonians 5: 17-18. In Ephesians 5: 20 he adds: 'always giving thanks to God the Father for everything, in the name of our Lord Jesus Christ.' In Phillipians 4: 6 he says: 'Do not be anxious about anything, but in everything, by prayer and petition, with thanksgiving, present your requests to God.' Finally, in Collossians 3: 17 we read: 'And whatever you do, whether in word or deed, do it all in the name of the Lord Jesus, giving thanks to God the Father through him.'

It is clear that we should thank God for the graces and blessings of life. It is good not to take them for granted, but rather to call them to mind with gratitude. But St Paul implies that we should also thank God for bad things, like illness, and personal sin. He says that it is God's will that we do so. How can we thank God for the misfortunes and sins in our lives? It is not that we thank God for these evils in themselves, but because we believe that they have been embraced by God's providence. Over the years I have come to realise that no matter what misfortunes I endure or what mistakes I make, they are integrated into God's plan for my life, and embraced by divine providence. So I firmly believe that, strange as it may seem, sin and suffering can become the birthplace of grace. Evil does not have the last word. That word belongs to God and it is a redeeming word of blessing and victory.

There is an outstanding biblical example of what I

mean. In the book of Genesis we are told that Joseph was the first child of Rachel and his father's favourite son. This is most clearly shown by the special coat that Jacob gave to Joseph. His older brothers hated him because he was their father's pet and because Joseph had dreams that he interpreted to his brothers in a rather conceited way. Joseph and his family were shepherds in the land of Canaan. One day Jacob sent Joseph to search for his brothers, who were tending the flocks. When Joseph found them, they seized upon the chance to kill him. The only opposing voice was Reuben's, so they compromised and sold Joseph into slavery.

Joseph was taken to Egypt. Psalm 105: 17-21 tells us that he was sold as a slave. After many adventures he rose to be minister of food in Egypt during a time of famine. The famine also struck Canaan, and Joseph's brothers eventually came to Egypt to buy grain. When they met Joseph he recognised them, but they failed to recognise him. Joseph was overcome with emotion. He revealed himself to them as their brother, whom they had sold into slavery years earlier. And he wept so loudly that the Egyptians heard him, and ....Joseph said to his brothers, 'I am Joseph! Is my father still living?' But his brothers were not able to answer him, because they were terrified at his presence. Then Joseph said to his brothers, 'Come close to me.' When they had done so, he said, 'I am your brother Joseph, the one you sold into Egypt! And now, do not be distressed and do not be angry with yourselves for selling me here, because it was to save lives that God

sent me ahead of you..... to preserve for you a remnant
on earth and to save your lives by a great deliverance.
'So then, it was not you who sent me here, but God'
Genesis 45: 2-8.

Joseph's statement is a remarkable one when you
think about it. God used the heartless treachery of his
brothers as the providential source of their future
blessing. There is an intimation in this story of the way
in which another brother would be delivered into the
hands of the chief priests and the Roman authorities
who would cruelly murder him. And just as Joseph's
suffering became a source of blessing for those who
inflicted it, so Jesus' suffering and death would become
the providential source of salvation and healing for
those who had caused it.

Amazing Grace

Surely this principle can be extended not only to our
sins but also to our sufferings. We can thank God *in* all
circumstances, rather than *for* all circumstances, in the
knowledge that they can become the springboards to
God's grace either sooner or later. I can remember an
occasion that occurred many years ago. I was due to
attend a conference for priests. I travelled to it by
motorbike. As I went along the road I was singing
hymns. At one point I prayed; 'Lord if you have any
message for the conference please speak to me.' Then I
felt inwardly that the Lord was saying, 'tell your fellow
priests about the pearl of great price.' While I was glad
to get that word, I didn't really know what it meant.
When I got to the conference there was a preparatory

prayer session. During a quiet time the image of an oyster came to mind. It was on the mud of the sea floor surrounded by water. I understood that the sea floor was the world, the sea the Spirit, and the oyster, the human person. Then I felt that the Lord was saying. 'Think of how a pearl is formed. Grit and dirt from the sea-bed get into the oyster. It cannot expel it. So it secretes a milky liquid which surrounds the grit over a seven year period. The greater the irritation the greater the pearl that is finally formed. It is the same with the human heart. The sin of the world makes an entry. But in my compassion I weave the pearl of mercy around it. The greater the sin, the greater the pearl that is finally formed. Tell the priests not to be disheartened by their weaknesses. I will bring good from evil, blessing from failure.' As St Paul proclaimed: 'where sin increased, grace increased all the more' Romans 5: 20.

Over the years I have found that the following prayer exercise is very beneficial. I think either of the greatest sin or the greatest misfortune in my life, or in the life of the community, e.g. church scandals. Then I express my negative feelings such as shame, humiliation, anger, guilt etc., but then I go on to express my faith conviction in prayers of thanksgiving. Like many others I have found that thanksgiving of this kind opens up my heart to the liberating power of God. I'm not surprised that Antony de Mello said that if he had to choose the one form of prayer that made Christ's presence most real in his life it would be the prayer of thanksgiving. He explained, 'The prayer consists, quite simply in thanking God for everything. It is based on the belief that nothing happens in our life that is not foreseen and planned by God – just nothing, not even our sins.' I'm sure that Merlin Carothers is correct when he says in his books such as *Prison to Praise* and *Power in Praise* that if, in adverse circumstances, we thank God in an unconditional way, the circumstances themselves can change in a remarkable manner.

Conclusion

Why not try this suggestion: Think of something in the past or present that is causing you pain, distress, guilt or frustration. If you are in any way to blame for this thing express your regret and sorrow to the Lord. Now explicitly thank God for this, praise the Lord for it...Tell God that you believe that even this fits into the divine plan for you and so God will draw great good from this for you and for others, even though you may not see the good. Leave this thing and all the other events of your life, past present and to come, in the hands of God and rest in the peace and relief that this will bring. As two Greek Orthodox writers observe: 'Lips forever giving thanks receive God's blessing, and a heart filled with gratitude unexpectedly receives grace.'

Chapter 7

Words of Knowledge

Jesus seemed to be able to read people's hearts and to predict future events. For instance, he seemed to know all about Nathaniel although he had never met him before (John 1:48), and he was able to tell the Samaritan woman that she hadn't one husband, but five (John 4:18). In the New Testament Church some of the believers were granted the same gift. For example, we are told that on one occasion the prophet Agabus: 'stood up and through the Spirit predicted that a severe famine would spread over the entire Roman world. This happened during the reign of Claudius' Acts 11:28.

Many of us have heard of contemporary charismatics such as Padre Pio, John Wimber, Briege McKenna, and Emilien Tardif who were blessed with 'words of knowledge.' They enabled them, in a supernatural way, to know hidden truths about people's lives. I suppose the person who was best known for this gift was the late Kathryn Kuhlman. The following words are taken from a transcript of one of her miracle services. 'There is a heart condition disappearing. Wonderful Jesus, I give you praise and glory. There is a case of sugar diabetes….the sugar is draining from your body….an ear has been opened completely. Someone hears me perfectly. In the balcony. Check on that someone. Up there in the top left balcony is a man with a hearing aid. Check that ear sir. Hold your good ear closed tight; you hear me perfectly.' Speaking about her exercise of this remarkable gift Kathryn said: 'My mind is so surrendered to the Spirit, that I know the exact body being healed; the sickness, the affliction, and in some instances the very sin in their lives. And yet I do not pretend to tell you why or how.'

New Testament Evidence

The most important New Testament reference to the word of knowledge is to be found in 1 Corinthians 12: 8 where St Paul says: 'To one there is given through the Spirit .... message of knowledge by means of the ... Spirit.' Most of the well known scholars who have commented on 1 Corinthians 12: 8, such as Carson, Kristemaker and Bittlinger, say that the word of knowledge refers to an inspired ability to preach and teach the good news. However, speaking of the charism of knowledge, Gordon Fee says in *God's Empowering Presence* that while the 'utterance of knowledge,' can take the form of inspired teaching, it can also refer to 'a supernatural endowment of knowledge, factual information that could not otherwise have been known without the Spirit's aid, such as frequently occurs in the prophetic tradition.' I was interested to see that Anglican bishop, David Pytches, endorses Fee's second interpretation. He states that the 'word of knowledge' is a: 'supernatural revelation of facts about a person or situation, which is not learned through the efforts of the natural mind, but is a fragment of knowledge freely given by God, disclosing the truth which the Spirit wishes to be made known concerning a particular person or situation.' In this article we will concentrate on this second interpretation.

Catholic Theology's Perspective

Catholic theology has long maintained that besides public revelation, which was completed with the death of the last apostle, there is also the possibility of private revelation. It takes the form of prophetic inspirations that are granted to particular individuals, such as the messages given by Our Lady to Catherine Laboure in the Rue de Bac. As such they are classified as mystical phenomena which are characteristic of the illuminative stage of the Christian life. St Thomas Aquinas describes some ways in which such enlightenment can be experienced: 'Now, accompanying this light that we have mentioned (i.e. of faith) which illumines the mind from within, there are at times in divine revelation other external or internal aids to knowledge; for instance, a spoken message, or something heard by the external senses which is produced by divine power, or something perceived internally through imagination due to God's action, or also some things produced by God that are seen in bodily visions, or that are internally pictured in the imagination. From these presentations, by the light internally impressed on the mind, man receives a knowledge of divine things.'

St Thomas seems to relate the gift of knowledge to the gift of prophecy. He says: 'Some charisms freely given relate to knowledge....Those relating to knowledge can be summed up in the word prophecy....Prophecy consists first and foremost in knowing certain far-off things outside the normal knowledge of men.... Prophetic knowledge relies on God's light in which all things are visible, human and divine, bodily and spiritual, so that anything whatever can be the subject of prophetic revelation. But secondarily it involves speech, since a prophet proclaims to others what God has taught him in order to build them up. And finally prophets sometimes work miracles to confirm their prophecies.'

In Catholic theology we say that grace builds on nature. Is there a natural gift upon which the supernatural gift, though distinct, depends?   It is not clear. Those who exercise this gift seem to be intuitive. But it could also be argued that they have a psychic gift that enables them to have extra sensory perception, perhaps by means of some kind of precognition, clairvoyance or telepathy. There are two problems with this theory, one scientific, the other theological. As far as empirical science is concerned there is no incontrovertible evidence to show that extra sensory perception (ESP) is a fact. Christian theology is opposed to all occult forms of knowledge and it tends to see ESP from this point of view. For example, par. 2116 of the *Catechism of the Catholic Church* is against consulting such things as clairvoyance in so far as they conceal a desire for power over time, history and, in the last analysis, other human beings. It seems to me, however, that the Church isn't against clairvoyance as such, but against the abuse of this ability.

Over the years I have found that that 'words of knowledge' can be received in different forms, such as an intuition, an inner word/s or an imaginative picture. However they are received, they can be invaluable in different ministry situations. Firstly, in the sacrament of reconciliation some priests will occasionally know a penitent's secret sins. This knowledge enables them to help him or her to make a good confession. Secondly, the Lord can guide intercessory prayer by means of a 'word of knowledge.' At a prayer meeting in Northern Ireland, for example, I heard a woman praying about a very specific trouble spot in Belfast. The next day we found out from the newspaper that at the very time she was praying, a car bomb had failed to go off in the exact location she had been concerned about. Thirdly, those who pray for inner healing are sometimes led by a 'word of knowledge' to focus on a repressed memory. A man who was suffering from claustrophobia went to a priest I know. After a few minutes of prayer he said 'you were nearly drowned when you were three.'

Immediately, the man recalled such a forgotten incident. Following a brief prayer, his phobia disappeared completely. Fourthly, as the ministry of Kathryn Kuhlman demonstrated, words of knowledge are sometimes granted to those praying for physical cures, particularly at healing services.

Conclusion

Not only do the four kinds of 'words of knowledge' guide the supplications and ministry of pray-ers, they also evoke the charism of expectant, unhesitating faith. As Jesus said: 'I tell you the truth, if anyone says to this mountain, 'Go, throw yourself into the sea,' and does not doubt in his heart but believes that what he says will happen, it will be done for him. Therefore I tell you, whatever you ask for in prayer, believe that you have received it, and it will be yours' Mark 11: 23-24. However, because of the ever present danger of illusions and false inspirations, it is important to exercise discernment of spirits in order to ascertain whether private revelations, one's own or those of others, truly come from God (cf 1 John 4:1).

Chapter 8

The Charism of Faith

The charism of faith is a neglected gift. In this chapter we will look at the nature of this attractive form of expectant trust, the motives we have of desiring it, and some practical means of receiving and exercising it.

What is the Charism of Faith?

The most important reference to this charism is to be found in 1 Corinthians 12: 9, where Paul says that to some is given, 'faith by the same Spirit.' Commentators down the centuries are agreed that Paul is not referring to saving faith, but rather to an exceptional form of expectant trust that leads to deeds of power. For example, St Thomas Aquinas says in his commentary on 1 Corinthians 12: 9 that the reference to

42

faith is not to be understood as the theological virtue of faith, i.e. saving faith, for that is common to all believers. Rather it is to be understood either as the expression of faith e.g. by means of inspired preaching and teaching, or as a special certitude of faith that leads to the working of healings and miracles.

Modern scripture scholars would agree with this interpretation. George Montague is representative of their shared opinion when he writes in his book *The Holy Spirit*, 'The gift of faith in 1 Corinthians12: 9 does not refer here to the faith that is necessary for salvation (Mark 16: 16; Hebrews 11: 6), but rather to a special intensity of faith for a specific need. Church of England bishop, David Pytches, accurately describes the charism of faith, in *Come Holy Spirit*, as, 'a supernatural surge of confidence from the Spirit of God which arises within a person faced with a specific situation of need whereby that person receives a trans-rational certainty and assurance that God is about to act through a word or action.'

It seems clear to me that the charism of expectant faith is evoked by charisms of revelation such as wisdom and knowledge, listed in 1 Corinthians 12: 8. They reveal what God's will is, in the here and now, e.g. by means of an inspiring word from scripture, a prophetic intuition, an interior picture, or word of knowledge, so a person has no lingering doubts about the promises of God. Once s/he knows God's existential will, they can pray either a prayer of intercession (Mark 11: 24) or command (Mark 11: 23) with complete assurance. As

1 John 5: 14 says, 'And this is the confidence we have in God, that if we ask for anything according to his will, he hears us. And if we know that he hears us in whatever we ask, we know that we have obtained the requests made of him.' In other words it is not a matter of praying with future hope, if what we ask for is in accordance with God's will. Rather, it is a matter of praying with present conviction because we already know that what we ask for is God's will. The charism of expectant faith is mainly expressed by means of the charisms of power listed in 1 Corinthians 12: 10 such as healing/exorcism and miracle working.

Why Should we Desire This Gift?

We know that Jesus did two main things in his ministry. Firstly, he proclaimed the Good News of God's unrestricted and unconditional mercy and love by means of inspired preaching and teaching. Secondly, he demonstrated the truth of the proclamation by the way he related to people, action for justice, and deeds of power such as healings, exorcisms and miracles. We should evangelise in the same way. Inspired preaching and teaching will not be enough. As Paul said: 'the kingdom of God does not consist in (mere) talk but in power' 1 Corinthians 4: 20. We also need to demonstrate the truth of our message in deeds, including deeds of power. Jesus promised, 'Very truly, I tell you, the one who believes in me will also do the works that I do, in fact, do greater works than these' John 14: 12. Before his ascension he added, 'These signs will accompany those who believe, by using my name they will cast out demons... they will lay their hands on the sick and they will recover' Mark 16: 17-18. There is clear evidence in the contemporary world that the only Christian groups, who are retaining the members they already have, and who are also gaining new members are those, such as Pentecostals, Charismatics and Evangelicals, who evangelise by means of inspired preaching and teaching, accompanied by deeds of power. Those deeds, as we have seen, are only made possible by the charism of faith.

A Testimony

Recently a Catholic woman in Northern Ireland told me that she was doing some shopping in a Protestant area. In one store, she happened to get into conversation with a fellow customer who told her that she was suffering from a painful physical problem. The Catholic woman was touched by what the afflicted woman had shared with her. She asked if she would like to be prayed with. The woman answered 'Yes,' so they went to a quiet, secluded part of the shop. As the Catholic woman prayed for her Protestant acquaintance she had a strong sense of God's love for her, and the Lord's desire, then and there, to help her by means of his healing power. The prayer lasted for only a few minutes, but it was full of care and conviction. Then the women parted, and returned to their respective homes.

A few days later the Protestant woman returned to the shop. She was looking for information about the person who had prayed for her, because in the interim she had been completely healed. She described what the mysterious stranger looked like. The shop keeper told her, to her complete surprise, that she was a Catholic woman, from a nearby town. Later, he contacted his Catholic customer to tell her the good news. Not surprisingly, when a Christian with expectant faith performs a deed of power for a member of another Church, not only does it manifest the presence and power of God's kingdom, it also tends to break down the dividing wall of division that sometimes separates Catholics from Protestants and visa versa.

How can we Acquire and Exercise the Charism of Faith?

1. Make love your aim and earnestly desire that some members of the Christian community will be graced with this charism (1 Corinthians 14: 1). This is done by means of private and public intercessory prayer.

2. St Cyril of Jerusalem said, as far as it depends on you, desire saving faith, which leads you to God, and you will receive the higher gift i.e. the charism of faith. In other words focus on the free, unmerited gift of God's saving mercy and love and all else will be added to you, including the charism of expectant faith.

3. St Paul tells us that faith comes by hearing the inspired and inspiring word of Christ (Romans 10:17). It is particularly important to focus on God's words of promise in scripture, the things that the Lord undertakes to do for those who trust, in an unhesitating way, in the divine assurances.

4. Associate with men and women of faith. Read testimonies and books which build up faith, e.g. the biographies of Kathryn Kuhlman.

5. Step out in faith, firstly in small things e.g. praying that a relative's headache will go away. Then go on to pray for greater things e.g. a cure of a friend's cancer or depression. Remember however, that we have to do so within the measure of faith the Lord has given us (Romans 12: 3). Over the years I have found that one can say a prayer of either intercession or command that lies half way between hesitant and unhesitating faith. Such a prayer is non-specific. While affirming in a general sense that God is at work in the situation it does not directly address a particular illness by telling it to go. As one prays in this way, hesitant trust can change into expectant faith.

Chapter 9

The Working of Miracles

When the Greek of 1 Corinthians 12: 10 is literally translated into English it says that to some is given 'operations of works of power.' However most translators use the shorter phrase 'the working of miracles.' The word 'miracle' comes from the Latin *miraculum*, meaning 'a wonder.' From a religious point of view a miracle is a supernatural manifestation of divine power which goes beyond the laws of nature, as we currently understand them, in such a way as to evoke religious awe and wonder in those who witness them. St Thomas Aquinas says 'The things God does when he by-passes the causes we know about we call miracles.'

We know that some of the great heroes of faith in the Old Testament performed miracles. For instance

Elijah raised a dead man, cured Naaman the leper, multiplied food and had God consume his sacrifice on Mount Carmel. In the New Testament, Jesus, the new Elijah, performed even greater miracles. He raised the dead, healed the sick, drove out demons, and performed nature miracles such as multiplying food, calming a storm and walking on water. He promised all those who believed in him, that they would perform even more impressive miracles 'greater works than these will they do, because I go to the Father,' John 14: 12. In the Acts we see that, like Jesus, 'many signs and wonders were done among the people by the hands of the apostles' Acts 5: 12.

Three kinds of miracle

Modern Catholics have been familiar with the working of miracles in three ways. Firstly, they are associated with great saints who performed them during their lives and after their deaths. For example, during his life, St Francis of Paola (1416-1507) of Calabria in Italy, was probably the greatest miracle worker the church has ever seen. He cured the sick, raised the dead, and it is said that he crossed the Straits of Messina by standing on his cloak which he laid upon the water. When saints die, one or two miracles are required for their canonisation. But, when St Charbel Makhlouf (1828-1898) a Maronite hermit from the Lebanon, was declared a saint in 1977, Pope Paul VI revealed that more first class miracles were submitted in support of his cause than for any other saint in history. As far as I can remember there were 1000 of them!

Secondly, miracles are associated with shrines like Lourdes. Its medical bureau applies criteria which were established in the 1700s by Pope Benedict XIV. He stipulated that in order to declare that a healing was miraculous it must be established that the disease was serious; that there was objective proof of its existence; that other treatments had failed; and that the cure was rapid, lasting and inexplicable from a scientific point of view.

The case of Gabriel Gargam is probably one of the best known of the cures at Lourdes. In December of 1899 a train on which he was travelling collided with another train. Gargam was thrown fifty two feet from his carriage. He was paralysed from the waist down. After eight months he had wasted away to a mere skeleton, weighing but seventy-eight pounds. His feet became gangrenous. He could take no solid food and was obliged to take nourishment by a tube. He was brought to Lourdes. He was carried to the pool and placed in its waters. The exertion caused him to collapse and he seemed to be dead. As the priest passed by with the monstrance, he pronounced a blessing over the covered body. Soon there was a movement from under the covering. To the amazement of the bystanders, the body raised itself to a sitting posture. While the family were looking on dumbfounded and the spectators gazed in amazement, Gargam said in a full, strong voice that he wanted to get up. They thought that it was a delirium before death, and tried to soothe him, but he was not to be restrained.   He got up and stood erect, walked a few paces and said that he was healed. On August 20th, 1901, sixty prominent doctors examined Gargam and pronounced him entirely cured.

Thirdly, there is the charism of miracle working.   In 1 Corinthians 12: 10 Paul says that in the Christian community it is possible that people could be gifted with the ability to perform occasional miracles. To understand his thinking correctly it is important to see this gift in the context of his theology of the community as the Body of Christ.   It is called to proclaim the Good News of the outpouring of God's unconditional mercy and love and to demonstrate its presence.   It does so, not only by means of loving relationships, deeds of mercy and action for justice, but in a specially striking way by means of deeds of power, such as healing, exorcism and miracle working. Like the performance of the other deeds of power, miracle working, whether in the form of inexplicable healing or changes in nature, depends upon the charism of expectant, unhesitating faith.   It is evoked in the heart by a revelation of God's purposes.   Whereas a healing assists and accelerates the body's natural potential for recovery, a miraculous healing goes well beyond what science thinks the auto-immune system is capable of achieving. There is reason to think that this unusual gift is associated in a special way with the ministry of being an apostle, prophet or teacher.

I have not seen too many miracles over the years.

However I can remember a time when a Polish man and a priest prayed for an English nun who was completely paralysed from the neck downward with multiple sclerosis. Following the prayer she recovered quickly. She was able to walk, drive and teach in school. It is very unlikely that it was a matter of profound remission because some twenty years later she has experienced no relapses. Because MS is untreatable, it is likely that the nun experienced a healing miracle.

Conclusion

Kathryn Kuhlman once wrote a book entitled, *I Believe in Miracles*. What makes that belief difficult for many in the modern world is the scientific world-view that says that miracles are impossible because the laws of nature are unchangeable. If miracles seem to occur they are explained away in scientific terms. Happily, nowadays a new scientific world-view is emerging. It maintains that nature is an open system where God can act in a miraculous way, by exploiting the potential of matter when it is influenced by the Holy Spirit as a result of the co-operation of faith-filled human beings.

Chapter 10

The Ministry of Deliverance

About a year ago I travelled to the UTV studios in Belfast to participate in a discussion on the existence or non-existence of the devil. For the sake of balance the producers tried, in typical fashion, to ensure that the participants represented three different world views. Briefly put, world-views are conscious and unconscious assumptions that govern our interpretation of reality.

• The programme included a psychiatrist who argued in naturalistic terms that there was neither God, devil, or supernatural realm. She explained them away, in psychological terms, as nothing but projections of the human mind.

• There was a liberal Christian academic who

accepted the existence of God, but explained away the devil as a mere myth that shouldn't be understood in literal, objective terms. The devil is another word for the evil effects of systemic injustice in the structures of society.

•   For my part, I tried to affirm the existence of a supernatural realm, including evil spirits, and therefore the possibility of exorcism. I may say that, as a result of a spiritual awakening many years before, I had moved from a liberal to a more traditional understanding of Christian teaching.

The Church's Position

A) Scriptural Evidence

It is clear from the New Testament that Jesus was an exorcist. The great scripture scholars of our day are all agreed on this. Jesus said in characteristic fashion: 'If it is by the finger of God that I cast out demons, then the kingdom of God has come upon you' Luke 11: 20. Years later in the post-resurrection era, St Peter testified: 'God anointed Jesus of Nazareth with the Holy Spirit and with power; he went about doing good and healing all that were oppressed by the devil, for God was with him' Acts 10: 38. Before he ascended into heaven, Jesus had given the disciples the authority to do the same. He said to them: 'These signs will accompany those who believe, in my name they will drive out demons' Mark 16: 17.

B) Church Teaching

Does the Church still teach that the devil exists? The

answer is yes, with certain qualifications. For example, Pope Paul VI said in an address: 'The question of the devil and the influence he can have on individual persons as well as communities, whole societies or events is a very important chapter of Catholic doctrine.... It is a departure from the picture provided by biblical and Church teaching to refer to the devil's existence.... as a pseudo reality, a conceptual and fanciful personification of the unknown causes of our misfortunes.' The Pope's views were echoed in *Christian Faith and Demonology*, published by the Vatican in 1975. It states: 'We repeat, ... that though still emphasising in our day the real existence of the demonic, the Church has no intention... of proposing an alternative explanation which would be more acceptable to reason. Its desire is simply to remain faithful to the Gospel and its requirements.'

At the launch of the revised rite of exorcism in late 1999, Cardinal Estevez, of the Congregation of Divine Worship, reiterated the Church's teaching, 'the existence of the devil is not an opinion... It belongs to Catholic faith and doctrine... but the strategy of the devil is to convince people that he does not exist.' The cardinal then went on to suggest that the Devil's malign activity helps to explain particular atrocities, such as Word War II and the Holocaust. He also stated in a more general way that the devil, 'manages to trap many people - he fools them by leading them to believe that happiness can be found in money, power and sexual lust. He deceives men and women by persuading them that they do not need God and that they are self-sufficient.'

C) Views of Eminent Scholars
The late Raymond Brown was one of the greatest biblical scholars writing in English in the post Vatican II era. He clearly stated in a number of his books, such as *An Introduction to the New Testament* (1997), that he believed that the devil exists and that Jesus was an exorcist. Karl Rahner the greatest Catholic theologian of the 20th century wrote: 'It should be firmly maintained that the existence of angels and demons is affirmed in scripture and not merely assumed as a hypothesis which can be dropped today.' While Catholic theology believes that the devil and evil spirits do exist, it would not be committed to the largely mythological cosmology of New Testament times.

Possession and Oppression

As regards the possibility of possession, the Catholic Church steers a middle course between a naturalistic denial of its possibility on the one hand, and a naïve, fundamentalist belief that possession is common, on the other. It makes a distinction between obsession and possession.

A) Obsession
When people are obsessed, they suffer from a spiritual neurosis where only part of their personality is subject to demonic influence. For instance, the devil can fill their minds with compulsive thoughts and evil inclinations, such as suicidal or murderous

inclinations. If I may say in passing, I have always thought that the violent and vicious activities of the paramilitaries in Northern Ireland had a demonic dimension. As Jesus said on one occasion, 'You are of your father the devil... he was a murderer from the beginning' John 8: 44.

B) Possession

When people are possessed, they suffer from a form of spiritual psychosis because the devil seems to take over their entire personalities. As a result they can have extraordinary physical strength which is inconsistent with their age or state of health, and also an ability to speak unknown languages and to discern hidden and distant things. While possession is theoretically possible, in actual fact, it is extremely rare. In the U.S. where there are over 40 million Catholics, there would only be a handful of genuine exorcisms a year. The vast majority of the bizarre behaviours which were once attributed to the devil can now be explained in medical and psychiatric ways, e.g. Tourette's syndrome which is a neurological disorder, characterised by tics, involuntary vocalisation, and often by the compulsive utterance of obscenities.

Forms of Deliverance

A) Solemn Exorcism

In the Catholic Church a solemn exorcism of a possessed person can only be performed by an exorcist who has been officially appointed by the bishop. I am not aware of any in Ireland at the present time, although there are many of them in other EU countries.

Let me give an example of what might be involved. A few years ago I witnessed a solemn exorcism. It was performed by an Irish priest living in England. He was the official exorcist of the diocese of Hexam and Newcastle. A woman asked for his help. Her presenting problem was a growth in her throat. She asked him for healing prayer. As he prayed she began to roar and scream in an unnatural way. Fr Sean pronounced the words of exorcism and she calmed down. Not only that, her lump disappeared. I met Sean a few years later and asked how the woman was getting on. He said that sadly she had neglected her spiritual life and that as a consequence her old problems had come back to haunt her.

Fr de Tonqedoc, a well known French exorcist once said 'Address the devil, and you will see him, or rather, not him but a portrait made up of the sick person's ideas of him.' This is what I call pseudo possession. I saw that vividly illustrated when I was ministering in Italy. The priest who had invited me to preach at a conference had a strong and naive belief in demonic influence. He also believed that he had the power to deal with it. This boosted his image and influence over the people. During the celebration of mass individuals would sometimes fall to the floor foaming at the mouth. Their psychiatric problems manifested themselves in terms of the priest's expectations which were shared by the congregation. This was confirmed by one particular case. An apparently possessed woman was brought for prayer by her husband and relatives. She was wrapped in a blanket. When she was uncovered she had a very strained and pale appearance. The local Italian priest felt that she needed an exorcism as did her family. He prayed over her for some time in a loud, booming voice, but his prayers seemed to have no effect. I strongly suspected that she wasn't possessed or oppressed but merely depressed. I asked to speak to her with the help of an interpreter. I told her, that God loved her. I asked her about her feelings and she confirmed that she was indeed suffering from depression and emotional upset. I prayed for inner healing, and all her psychosomatic agitation ceased and she became completely peaceful. She remained that way afterwards.

B) Simple Exorcism

Simple exorcisms can be performed by any believer in cases where a person is obsessed, rather than possessed by the devil. A number of years ago I performed one when I was working in an Irish hospital. One evening I gave holy communion to a girl of twelve, who sometime before had a tumour removed from her brain. The next day, I met her again and she told me she was under the influence of an evil spirit. She said that it all started when she began reading people's palms and found that she could tell them about their past and future. Some time later she was disturbed by apparitions of her dead grandmother. My first reaction was one of intuitive belief. It was quickly followed by a more rational type of incredulity. It was hard to believe that such a young girl could be oppressed by an evil spirit. I presumed that there was some psychological or physical explanation for her state of mind.

I had many conversations with Mary and discovered that although she was only twelve, she was endowed with a maturity and intelligence, way beyond her years. I also talked with people who knew her and discussed her case with a neurologist, a psychiatrist, a number of priests, two experienced exorcists, and a theologian who was familiar with this kind of problem. After a two month discernment process, a consensus emerged. The facts were pointing toward the probability of oppression by an evil spirit. The theologian encouraged me to anoint Mary. I told him that she had already been anointed prior to an operation some time before. However, her problem had persisted. He said it wasn't surprising, because the priest who performed the anointing hadn't known anything about her spiritual oppression. So he encouraged me to anoint her again and to perform a simple exorcism by praying silently for deliverance during the laying-on of hands.

I told Mary of my intention. Meantime I prepared by prayer and fasting and enlisted the supportive prayers of a couple of other people. Finally, the time of the anointing arrived. When I reached the ward, I was delighted when this strange and remarkable girl informed me of her own accord that she was willing to give up the occult for good. I promised her that when I put my hands on her head the evil would go away and that she would be filled with the Holy Spirit. He would protect her from evil in the future. She replied with startling clarity, 'I have trusted my mother for her love, my doctor for my life; now I trust you for my soul.' I assured her that Jesus wouldn't let her down, with more confidence than I actually felt. Then I proceeded by celebrating the sacrament of reconciliation. After giving her absolution I moved on to the sacrament of anointing. During the laying-on of hands, I prayed silently, 'In the name of Jesus, I command the spirit of the occult, and any other spirit that may be disturbing you, to yield to the power and the will of God.' Because I was morally certain that I was praying within the will of God, I had a growing conviction that what I was asking was already being granted. I concluded the prayer by requesting the Lord to fill Mary's soul with the light, peace and protection of the Holy Spirit.

When I went home that night, I asked the Lord to confirm whether the deliverance had been successful or not. The next day, when I returned to the ward around noon, I discovered that, unexpectedly, my young friend had been released earlier that morning. I was grateful to divine providence that I had managed to anoint her in the nick of time, just before her departure. As I stood there, a middle aged woman beckoned to me. When I got to her bedside she said, 'You know Mary who was in the bed opposite; she went home at nine this morning. Father, I want to tell you something. I have seen a lot of life, and I wouldn't say this lightly. I know that Mary was young, but there was something peculiar, even sinister about her.' 'Why would you say that?' I asked. 'Well, Father,' she replied, 'Just take one example. Some time ago, about four of us were due for surgery. We had a bottle of Lourdes water and we all blessed ourselves with it. But when we offered it to her, she recoiled in horror. You should have seen the look on her face. It wasn't normal. But something must have happened recently, because this morning she asked me for the Lourdes water. When I gave it to her, she went over to her own bed and blessed herself from head to toe. Not only that, she was changed somehow. The sense of evil was gone. And by the way she left a letter for you.' I said goodbye to the woman and went off thanking God for this indication that the prayer for deliverance had been answered. This impression was confirmed when I read Mary's memorable words. She said that all her occult powers had left her as a result of the anointing. They had been replaced by an inward sense of God's presence and peace.

C) Deliverance of Places from Disturbing Influences
The notion of the exorcism or deliverance of places is a related but controversial issue. It has to do with haunted houses where there are strange noises, images and disturbing happenings. Fr Martin Israel, an Anglican priest, psychiatrist and exorcist, and Frank McNutt a Catholic exorcist believe that places can sometimes suffer from demonic infestation and need prayer for cleansing and deliverance. I dealt with such a case last year in Northern Ireland. A family contacted me through their bishop. I also think that Rev Billy Lendrum when he says that sometimes disturbances in houses may be caused by the restless

spirits of the dead, which for one reason or another need our help to go to God. For many years they had been aware of a child crying and the footsteps of a man walking across the floor in the upstairs rooms. The disturbances had become so bad that the family had ended up living downstairs. The noises were getting worse and it was having an upsetting effect on everyone.

I told the mother by phone that there was need for a diagnosis, that is, a cause proportionate to the disturbance. Shortly before I was due to visit the family, the mum, who is a part time hairdresser, was told by a client that a child had been abused by a man some fifty years before in the house. This was the information we needed. When I got to the house I had a chat with the family, told them what I intended to do, and then invited them to join me in prayer. I commended the spirits of the child and the man to the mercy and peace of God. I blessed the rooms with blessed water and salt. Happily, the problem seemed to cease after that. Whether this was a prayer of exorcism or healing I'm not sure, but it amounted to a sort of deliverance.

The Way Forward

Clearly discernment of spirits is essential when dealing with people who suspect that they are either obsessed or possessed by evil. To do so effectively, Christians need to have a knowledge of abnormal psychology as well as spirituality. If they don't have such knowledge themselves they need to consult those who have. If it is established that besides having a possible psychological problem, a person is obsessed by evil, any priest or lay person can pray with expectant faith that the afflicted individual will be delivered by the Spirit of God. If perchance, a person has been the victim of the 'evil eye' or a curse, the Church clearly states that prayer for deliverance rather than exorcism is appropriate. In the very rare cases, where exorcism is actually necessary, the Church's latest document on exorcism indicates how it should be conducted, e.g. by means of prayer, the use of holy water, the laying on of hands and a blessing with a crucifix.

Conclusion

All of us need to question the post Enlightenment world view that excludes the supernatural realm. As Pope Pius XII once remarked, the Devil's greatest lie is to have people believe that he doesn't exist. For its part, the Irish Church could respond to the new rite of exorcism by appointing an exorcist in every diocese, in line with par. 1172 of the *Code of Canon Law*. Then if people are worried about some paranormal incident, or suspect that someone is either obsessed or possessed by evil they could be referred, if needs be, to the official exorcist. Finally, all of us need to remind ourselves of the prophetic words of John Paul II in 1979, 'Satan, the tempter, the adversary of Christ, will use all his might and all his deceptions to win Ireland for the way of the world…. Pray that Ireland may not fail in the test. Pray as Jesus taught us to pray: 'Lead us not into temptation but deliver us from evil."

Chapter 11

*Did Mother Teresa Need
an Exorcism?*

On September 5th 2001, many people commemorated the 4th anniversary of the death of Mother Teresa of Calcutta. Pope John Paul II has already introduced her cause for canonisation. Part of the process includes the collection of relevant documentation. As a result, Teresa's private letters have been gathered and extracts published in an obscure magazine. They reveal, that all had not been sweetness and light in the life of the 'messiah of love.' While her public utterances were beautiful, uplifting and positive, her private correspondence, especially in the 1950's and 60's, indicates that she often experienced desolation of spirit, and severe temptations against faith.

Revelatory Letters

For example, Teresa encouraged people to have firm trust in God. She said on one occasion: 'Faith is a gift of God. Without it there would be no life. And our work, to be fruitful and to be all for God, and beautiful, has to be built on faith, faith in Christ.' It might come as a surprise to find that she wrote privately to her spiritual advisor: 'People say they are drawn close to God, seeing my strong faith. Is this not deceiving people? Every time I have wanted to tell the truth, that I have no faith, the words just do not come, my mouth remains closed. And yet I still keep on smiling at God and all.'

With good reason we think of Mother Teresa as a woman of fervent prayer. She said in characteristic fashion: 'Love to pray. Feel often during the day the need for prayer, and take trouble to pray. Prayer enlarges the heart until it is capable of containing God's gift of himself.' But in her own life she sometimes found prayer to be well nigh impossible. In one letter she wrote: 'When I try to raise my thoughts to heaven, there is such utter emptiness that those very thoughts return like sharp knives and hurt my very soul. I want God with all the power of my soul, and yet between us there is terrible separation. I don't pray any longer.'

Mother Teresa believed that the Lord's disciples should be willing to give generously to God, especially, by means of loving acts of service. Speaking about her order and its co-workers she said: 'The spirit of our society is total surrender, loving trust and cheerfulness.' But she disclosed in a letter that, she often found the demands of unstinting generosity very difficult. 'In my soul,' she wrote, 'I can't tell you how dark it is, how painful, how terrible, I feel like refusing God. Pray for me that I may not refuse God in this hour, I don't want to do it but I am afraid I may do it. Pray for me.'

Finally, speaking about the divine indwelling she said on one occasion: 'A Christian is a tabernacle of the living God.' But in her private sharings she wrote: 'The child of God's love has now become as the most hated one, the one he has thrown away unloved. I call, I cling, I want, but there is no answer... I am told God lives in me, and yet the reality of darkness and coldness and emptiness is so great that nothing touches my soul, between us there is a terrible separation.'

Mother Teresa Exorcised

Around the same time that the letter extracts were being made public, many newspapers and magazines revealed that, about a year before her death, on Sept 5th 1997, the devil rather than God seemed to be the one touching Mother Teresa's soul. And so she had to be exorcised! This disclosure, surprised some, and shocked many. In an interview, the Archbishop of Calcutta, Henry D'Souza described the controversial incident which occurred, in 1996, one year before Mother Teresa's death at the age of 87. Providentially, the Archbishop and Mother Teresa happened to be patients in the same hospital at the same time. Each of them underwent angioplasty to relieve cardiac problems. Teresa's distress occurred during the recuperative period. Evidently, she became extremely agitated at night. She was unable to sleep, tossed and turned and tried to pull off the drips and monitoring wires that were attached to her arms and body.

In the judgement of the doctors, there was no natural explanation for Mother's behaviour. We can only presume that they had taken into account the fact that many elderly people can react in this way as a result of anxiety, depression or the side-effects of medication. Evidently, in Mother Teresa's case the doctors had also ruled out the possibility that the dye, which was used in the preparatory angiogram had caused her to become very agitated. It is an established fact that the use of such a contrast medium in the circulatory system can sometimes have this effect. However, it was unlikely that any of these possible causes of her restlessness would have been active at night time only. Archbishop D'Souza took the doctors at their word. In the light of what they said, he concluded that Teresa was possibly under spiritual attack by the devil. He said: 'It struck me that there could be some evil spirit which was trying to disturb her.... because of her weakened physical condition.'

In the course of an interview D'Souza said: 'I wanted her to calm down and asked a priest an old Italian missionary who was very holy... in the name of the church, to perform an exorcism prayer on her.' Apparently, the priest in question was a 79 year old

Sicilian, named Rosario Stroscio. D'Souza said to the priest: 'Please say the prayer of exorcism over Mother Teresa.' He got a shock and replied, 'Should I drive out the devil if it is there?' The Archbishop said to him, 'You command the devil to go if he is there. In the name of the church, as archbishop, I command you to go and do it.' Although Mother Teresa hadn't said that she felt under attack by the devil, apparently she was happy about the archbishop's proposal and willingly co-operated with the prayer which lasted for about half an hour. The Archbishop explained that, in the event, a solemn exorcism to expel the devil from Mother Teresa's personality had not been necessary. Instead a prayer for protection from the attacks of the evil one had been said. The Archbishop believed it had been effective because, from then on, the night time agitation ended and Teresa was able to sleep in peace.

Archbishop D'Souza is a learned, and experienced pastor. Having assessed the situation, he instinctively concluded that, due to her physical weakness and vulnerability, Mother Teresa could be attacked by the enemy of her soul. Clearly, the prelate was operating out of a supernatural world view. Unlike many people nowadays, who think that the devil is merely a symbolic word for the dark side of the human unconscious, the oppressive structures of society, or the sum total of human evil; he believes that the Devil exists. He also accepts, in a traditional Catholic way, that he can and does exercise a malign influence on people's lives especially the lives of exceptionally holy people.

The word exorcism needs some explanation. As a number of experts have pointed out, there are two forms, solemn and simple. Solemn exorcism is conducted in a public way by a priest appointed by the local bishop. It seeks to drive out the evil spirit from the personality of someone who is inwardly possessed. Simple exorcism can be conducted in private by any believing Christian. It seeks to deliver the personality from outward oppression, obsession and harassment by the devil. Although the exorcism conducted by Fr Stroscio was carried out in the name of the church in a public way, it was really a simple exorcism which sought to deliver Mother Teresa from diabolical obsession. The word obsession comes from the Latin *obsidere* meaning, 'to sit before, to besiege a stronghold.' Of course, having first laid siege, the devil can then seek to enter the stronghold of the personality through some breach in its walls. The Archbishop had this possibility in mind. By means of a prayer of simple exorcism the prelate sought to end the siege and to protect Mother from attack.

Some time after the reports of Mother Teresa's exorcism, Fr Amorth, the chief exorcist in the diocese of Rome confirmed this point. He cited the example of Blessed Padre Pio and St John Vianney who were both harassed, though not possessed by the evil one. Then he went on to make the remarkable claim that 'many holy people have been possessed' such as Sr. Maria of Jesus Crucified who was born in Galilee in 1846. 'There were two periods in her life,' Fr. Amorth said, 'in which she was possessed and needed to have exorcisms.' She died in Bethlehem in 1878 and was the first Arab to be beatified in 1988. Something similar happened in the life of St Gemma Galgani. She was born in 1878 and was known to behave in a bizarre way that she herself attributed to diabolical possession. She died in 1903.

Was An Exorcism Necessary?

It is clear that, in Mother Teresa's case, Archbishop D'Souza decided to err on the side of caution by instructing Fr. Stroscio to conduct an exorcism. Whether this was the prudent thing to do is open to question. Not everyone will be convinced that an exorcism was really needed. It could be argued that Mother Teresa herself didn't ask for such a prayer. Furthermore those who write in a well informed way about spiritual oppression and obsession, such as Jordan Aumann in *Spiritual Theology*, or Francis McNutt in *Deliverance From Evil Spirits*, don't mention physical agitation as a typical sign of demonic activity. It could be argued that Mother Teresa's doctors shouldn't have ruled out a psychosomatic explanation for her disturbed behaviour as quickly as they did. For his part, the bishop could have encouraged Fr Stroscio to engage in a more careful and measured process of discernment, as the church's official documents recommend. He could have advocated a more graduated approach which would have begun by using some of the more ordinary means of ministry such as healing prayer accompanied by a blessing with either holy water, blessed salt, or the oil of gladness. It is also surprising that he didn't ask the priest to administer the sacrament of the anointing of the sick and to pray that God would protect Mother Teresa from the wiles of the devil. This could have been done during the extension of the priest's hands over her head. Then, if all else failed, Fr Stroscio could have concluded by pronouncing a prayer of simple exorcism.

Teresa and Therese

As I read the extracts from Mother's Teresa's letters I couldn't help seeing parallels between her experience and that of her namesake, Therese of Lisieux. Indeed she once said: 'I haven't called myself after the big Teresa (of Avila), but after the little one, Teresa (Therese) of Lisieux.' It is interesting to note that Teresa of Calcutta, endured similar spiritual trials as Therese of Lisieux. To give just a couple of examples. In her *Autobiography*, Therese talked about voices, ...who seemed to say in mocking tones: 'It is all a dream, this talk of a heavenly country, bathed in light, scented with delicious perfumes, and of a God who made it all, who is to be our possession in eternity!... All right, all right, go on longing for death! But death will make nonsense of your hopes; it will only mean a darker night than ever, the night of mere non-existence and annihilation.' A companion of Therese, Sister St. Augustine, reported: 'She admitted something to me which surprised and confused me, 'If only you knew the darkness into which I've been flung! I don't believe in eternal life; I think, after this life there will be nothing more. Everything has vanished for me.'

Spiritual writers maintain that this kind of desolation of spirit, sometimes referred to as the dark night of the soul, is allowed by God for a purpose. The Lord withdraws spiritual consolation, all feeling of the divine presence, in order to purify the person. Having learned to focus on the God of consolation rather than the consolations of God, St Ignatius of Loyola says that mature souls sometimes experience a kind of spiritual depression because: 'The Lord does not want people to rise up in spirit in a certain pride and vainglory and attribute to themselves the devotion and other effects of spiritual consolation.' The Carmelite tradition maintains that the vicissitudes which were experienced by the two Teresas, were intended by God to purify their inner senses. They were calculated to teach them to let go of inadequate concepts and images of God, together with their attendant feelings. They were being led to commit their wills in a loving way, without the aid of mind or imagination, to the One who lives in the darkness of a cloud of unknowing.

In another striking parallel, Therese of Lisieux, like Mother Teresa was attacked by the devil, when she was a child of ten, when she suffered from terrible headaches and convulsions, and again shortly before her death. On the day she died, September 30th 1897, Therese suffered such violent temptations against faith that she was in total darkness. Several hours before her death, perspiration stood out on her forehead. She was very agitated, close to despair and asked the sisters to sprinkle holy water on her. Her sister Pauline, i.e. Mother Agnes, was bewildered. She went and prayed before a statue, saying, 'Oh Sacred Heart of Jesus, I beg you, do not let my sister die in despair.' In a way it wasn't surprising that Therese was suffering in this way. She had stated in the past that she had asked to die the death of Jesus on the cross. It would seem then, that the two Teresas often shared in Christ's feeling of being abandoned by God and harassed by the evil one.

Conclusion

When asked whether the exorcism would hinder the cause for Mother Theresa's beatification, the Archbishop said no - like the extracts from the letters - it would have the opposite effect. He stated that: 'it would be an indication of the holiness of Mother.' In the Christian life, it is common for the saintly friends of God to be attacked in this way. As Sirach 2: 1 warns: 'My child, if you desire to serve the Lord, prepare yourself for an ordeal.' It would seem that Mother Teresa had been allowed to share in Christ's feeling of being abandoned by God and harassed by the evil one. Like her Saviour, she triumphed with God's help, over every adversity (cf. Romans 8: 36-39). We can leave the final word to Sr Nirmala, Teresa's successor: 'Today Mother is with God. Now in his presence, she has more power with God. She is no more on an earthly level. She has passed to eternal life. There she is very, very powerful.'

Chapter 12

The Gift of Prophecy

In theory the gift of prophecy has been important since the beginnings of the Charismatic Movement. In practice, however it has often been neglected, misunderstood, or abused. For example, when I attend prayer meetings and conferences I am sometimes disappointed by the absence of genuine prophecy. When people have spoken prophetic messages I have often suspected that they were merely expressing pious sentiments in prophetic terms. For example, I once heard a man say: 'My people I wana to tell you, that I love yis all!' It was true, I'm sure, but was it prophecy? On a few occasions I have heard false prophecies that were opposed to charity or the teachings of scripture and the Church. When one such prophecy was spoken at an international conference, I heard the Rev Tom Smail hit the table with his fist and say: 'Stop at once, that's a false prophecy!' This brief chapter will examine the nature and role of authentic prophecy, the motives we have for desiring it, while suggesting some practical means of receiving and exercising this important gift.

The nature of prophecy

The word 'prophet' is derived from the Greek *prophetes*, meaning interpreter, or spokesman. In other words a prophet or prophetess is a person who speaks or acts, in a revelatory way on God's behalf, under the inspiration of the Holy Spirit. In his commentary on 1 Corinthians 12: 10, St Thomas Aquinas said in the *Summa Theologica*: 'In a broad sense the subject of prophecy is whatever man knows by God's revelation. It differs from other charisms such as wisdom and knowledge and understanding of speech, the subjects of which man can know by natural reason, though not as perfectly as by God's light.... Prophecy is knowledge imprinted on the prophet's mind by the teaching of *God's revelation* (my italics).' In the *Summa Contra Gentiles*, Thomas described how such knowledge can be imparted by God: 'Now, accompanying this light that we have mentioned which illumines the mind from within, there are at times in divine revelation other external or internal aids to knowledge; for instance, a spoken message, or something heard by the external senses which is produced by divine power, or something perceived internally through imagination due to God's action, or also some things produced by God that are seen in bodily visions, or that are internally pictured in the imagination. From

76

these presentations, by the light internally impressed on the mind, man receives a knowledge of divine things.' Thomas also said that prophecy is primarily a 'divine revelation, announcing future events with unshakeable truth.' As such it is akin to what Charismatics refer to as a 'word of knowledge' which is a supernatural gift of knowledge or factual information that could not otherwise have been known without the Spirit's aid. It frequently occurred in the Old and New Testament prophetic tradition.

Modern scripture scholars say that prophecy is more a matter of 'forth-telling' than 'fore-telling.' In other words the prophet or prophetess evaluates the signs of the times in terms of the mind and heart of God. They gain this insight as a result of an inspired vision, inner word, or dream. Although genuine prophecy is revelatory, it merely elucidates the implications of scriptural revelation, without adding to it.

Motives for desiring the gift

Rather than being a sign of the holiness of the prophet or prophetess, the gift of prophecy is freely granted in order to help others to grow in sanctifying grace. As Paul says in 1 Corinthians 14: 3: 'everyone who prophesies speaks to men for their edification, exhortation and comfort.' There are a number of ways in which prophecy does this.

Firstly, it can take the form of a message which is spontaneously inspired by the Holy Spirit and spoken into a particular situation. For example, in recent years a prophecy has been widely circulated in the Charismatic Movement. What is unusual about it is the fact that it was delivered by Smith Wigglesworth (1859-1947), an English Evangelical who was renowned for his prayer life and strong faith. In the year of his death he predicted three interventions of the Holy Spirit.

'During the next few decades there will be two distinct moves of the Holy Spirit across the Church in Great Britain. The first move will affect every church that is open to receive it and will be characterised by a restoration of the baptism and gifts of the Holy Spirit.

'The second move of the Holy Spirit will result in people leaving historic churches and planting new churches.

'In duration of each of these moves, the people who are involved will say 'This is the great revival.' But the Lord says 'No,' neither is this the great revival, but both are steps towards it.

'When the new church phase is on wane, there will be evidenced in the churches something that has not been seen before: a coming together of those with an emphasis on the Word and those with an emphasis on the Spirit.

'When the Word and the Spirit come together, there will be the biggest movement of the Holy Spirit that the nation, and indeed the world has ever seen. It will mark the beginning of a revival that will eclipse anything that has ever been witnessed within these shores, even the Wesleyan and Welsh revivals of former years. The outpouring of God's Spirit will flow over from the U.K. to the mainland of Europe, and from there will begin a missionary move to the ends of the earth.'

Secondly, prophecy can take the form of inspired and inspiring preaching based on a scripture text. I can recall a memorable talk given by David Pawson, a British evangelical leader entitled, 'It is not fair.' It was about the parable of the labourers in the vineyard (Matthew 20: 1-16) and was prophetic in its impact upon me personally.

Thirdly, prophecy can take the form of a challenging public pronouncement on a moral or ethical issue that confronts current social values. I felt that part of John Paul II's address in Limerick, in 1979, about the dangers of materialism and the coming time of testing in Ireland, was prophetic in this sense.

Fourthly, one can either receive a personal word interiorly or through someone else. For example I heard these prophetic words many years ago.

'I do not despise you imperfection. I live in it. When you see the flaws in your brothers and sisters, and the wounds in your own heart, do not feel that they will separate you from me. I live in those wounds. I reveal myself through your brokenness. When you look at the cross you do not see a perfect Lord, but a broken one. You do not see light but darkness. You do not see joy, but anguish and pain. My child I have descended into the depths of your imperfection, there to reveal the glory of my Father. For I love you in your brokenness, and you run away from it, as if it were not acceptable to me, as if I would despise it. It is my treasure. My light shines forth in all that you fear. So look to it. Accept it, in the knowledge that I am within it. You will learn to see me in places you have never seen me before and in a world that frightens you today. You will see my face shining through tomorrow, for you will have changed, you will see as I see, my glory is everywhere.'

I received the following prophetic message from a Protestant woman I knew.

'My son, too long you have remained imprisoned by the thoughts and traditions of men and your fear of them, but I am calling you forth into a new place with me. The training I have given you, the dark places through which I have led you, have been but a preparation for far greater things yet. You praise me because of the blessings I have already given you, but this has been but a paddling in the shallows compared with what I wish to do through you, as I call you out to walk on the water with me. It will not be an easy walk my son, but I know your commitment to me and your desire to serve me, so all I ask of you is that you trust me.'

The Gift of Prophecy

Means of Acquiring the Gift

St Paul esteemed the gift of prophecy very highly. He ranked it second after apostleship (Ephesians 4: 11). It is the two edged sword that judges the secret thoughts and emotions of the heart (Hebrews 4: 12). As Paul says: 'if an unbeliever or someone who does not understand comes in while everybody is prophesying, he will be convinced by all that he is a sinner …. So he will fall down and worship God, exclaiming, 'God is really among you!' (1 Corinthians 14: 24-25.) Like Moses before him Paul wished that everyone could prophesy (1 Corinthians 14: 39). As a result he exhorted the believers to desire this gift. 'Follow the way of love,' he wrote (1 Corinthians 14: 1) 'and eagerly desire spiritual gifts, especially the gift of prophecy.' This desire can be advocated and encouraged in a number of ways.

1. The group leader should arrange for good teaching to be given on this gift. It is interesting to note that St Thomas saw it as the key to a proper understanding of all the other charisms.
2. S/he should encourage the prayer group members to ask God, with expectant faith, to grant the gift of prophecy to one or more of the members.
3. The prayer group leader needs to adopt a permissive attitude where prophecies are concerned. While there will be quite a few non-prophecies, s/he should not bother too much about them. They won't do any real harm. The charism of discernment of spirits, which is mentioned in 1 Corinthians 12: 10, is needed to distinguish genuine prophecy from non prophecy or

false prophecy.

4. I have also discovered that the Lord is more liable to grant the gifts, especially the charism of prophecy, when the group members are one in mind and heart (Cf. Phillipians 2: 1-4; Acts 4: 32). This means that they have to resolve conflicts in a constructive and forgiving way, while fasting from judgmental or condemnatory thoughts or words. I have also noticed that groups that are committed to vociferous praise, that is loud and long, especially in tongues, are more disposed to receive the gift of prophecy.

Means of Exercising the Gift

When it comes to the exercise of prophecy a number of points should be kept in mind.

• Firstly, 'If a person's gift is prophesying, let him or her use it in proportion to his or her faith' Romans 12: 6. If one's faith is hesitant speak in a tentative way, such as, 'I feel that the Lord may be saying.' If it is firm, one could say, 'The Lord says....'
• Secondly, 'Two or three prophets should speak, and the others should weigh carefully what is said' (1 Corinthians 14: 29.) In other words the leader should only allow a few prophetic messages to be spoken. If a genuine prophecy is uttered, the leader would be well advised to encourage the group to absorb its meaning by means of quiet, prayerful, reflection.
• Thirdly, 'You can all prophesy in turn so that everyone may be instructed and encouraged' (1 Corinthians 12: 31.) Clearly, Paul thought that good order in the meeting is important with pauses between

the prophecies.

• Fourthly, I feel that someone should be assigned to write down genuine prophecies after the meeting so they can be referred to again. Remember, that Isaiah 55: 11 assures us, the word of God will not return to the Lord without accomplishing the purpose for which it was sent.

• Fifthly, if God speaks a word to a group or community, they need to take that word to heart and to respond to it in an obedient way. As Jesus said: 'Blessed are those who hear the word of God and keep it' (Like 11:28.) Otherwise, when, finally, we go before God's judgement seat we will say: 'Lord, Lord, did we not prophesy in your name' and he will reply: 'I never knew you. Away from me, you evildoers!' (Matthew 7: 22-23.)

Chapter 13

Is Prophecy About Catastrophe or Hope?

Albert Nolan's book, *Jesus Before Christianity*, begins with a section entitled, 'Catastrophe.' In the first chapter he says that, rather than being a prediction, a prophecy is a warning or a promise. Then he goes on to show how John the Baptist was a true prophet in this sense. He maintained that the Jewish people had reached a point of crisis. He appealed to people from all walks of life to give up their former sins and turn wholeheartedly to God. Nolan goes on to make the interesting assertion that the baptism of Jesus, by John, was tantamount to a positive acceptance of his basic contention. However, Jesus maintained that if the people repented, the sudden turn for the worse could be averted.

There are a number of texts such as Luke 21: 20-23; and 23: 28 in which Jesus spoke about forthcoming tribulations of Israel. For example in Luke 12: 54 - 3: 5, Jesus said that although people were well able to predict when the weather was going to change, they were unable to discern the signs of the times, from a political and religious point of view. He then went on to refer to two traumatic experiences; the way in which Pilate mingled the blood of Galileans he had massacred with the blood of the temple sacrifices, and the loss of eighteen lives when the tower of Siloam fell on them. Then Jesus commented that the victims had not been singled out for punishment. They were no more sinful than anyone else. But then he warned in a typically prophetic way: 'I tell you, if you do not repent, you will all perish as they did. In Luke 19: 43-44 he intimated what form the impending catastrophe could take, when he said: 'A time is coming when your enemies will raise fortifications all around you, when they will encircle you and hem you in on every side; they will dash you and your children inside your walls to the ground; they will leave not one stone standing on another within you – and all because you did not recognise your opportunity when God offered it!'

It would seem probable, then, that Jesus prophesied the destruction of Jerusalem by the Romans. However it wasn't inevitable. If the people, like those of Nineveh in Jonah's time, accepted the Good News message about the in-breaking of the reign of God, and turned back to God in response, disaster could be averted. However, if the people failed to respond, the forces of evil would inevitably take their destructive course. No wonder there was such a sense of urgency in the preaching of Jesus. Is it any surprise that he wept over Jerusalem (Luke 19: 41), when he could see that the chosen people were not responding to the gospel message. As we know, the Lord's prophecy was fulfilled a few years after his death and resurrection. In 70 AD the Romans destroyed Jerusalem, demolished the Temple and murdered over a million people.

Scripture scholars suggest that the destruction of the holy city became a metaphor for the tribulations that would precede the end times (Cf 2 Thessalonians 2: 1-12). As a result, there has been an apocalyptic dimension to Christian theology down through the centuries. At its best, it involves a prophetic sense of the need for on-going conversion to the gospel as the best way of avoiding all kinds of impending misfortunes. In recent years, there have been many people, for example, in the ranks of Pentecostalism and Catholic Popular Piety who have claimed to have received messages from God. They usually say something like 'pray and repent for otherwise great chastisement will come upon the world.'

Visionaries Warn about Possible Disasters

For more than a century now, a number of visionaries have made dire predictions. Here are just four of many possible examples. Following an apparition at La Salette in France, in 1846, one of the visionaries wrote:

'The Church will be in eclipse, the world will be in dismay. But now Enoch and Eli will come, filled with the Spirit of God. They will preach with the might of God, and men of good will shall believe in God, and many souls will be converted. They will make great steps forward through the virtue of the Holy Spirit and will condemn the devilish lapses of the Antichrist. Woe to the inhabitants of the earth! There will be bloody wars and famines, plagues and infectious diseases.'

The second secret of Fatima, which was revealed in 1917, warned: 'This war is going to end, but if people do not cease offending God, not much time will elapse and during the Pontificate of Pius XI another and more terrible war will begin. When you see a night illuminated by an unknown light, know this is the great sign from God that the chastisement of the world for its many transgressions is at hand through war, famine, persecution of the Church and of the Holy Father.'

In 1973, Sister Agnes Katsuko Sasagawa, of Akita Japan, claimed that among other things the Blessed Virgin Mary had said: 'In order that the world might know His anger, the Heavenly Father is preparing to inflict a great chastisement on all mankind. With my Son, I have intervened so many times to appease the wrath of the Father. I have prevented the coming of calamities by offering Him the sufferings of the Son on the Cross, His Precious Blood, and beloved souls who console Him and form a cohort of victim souls. Prayer, penance and courageous sacrifices can soften the

Father's anger.'

Thomas Petrisko's *The Sorrow, The Sacrifice and The Triumph* is about controversial Irish visionary, Christina Gallagher. It contains many of the revelations she claims to have received. Among them are messages she passed on in the early 1990's: 'The world is in great danger. It is on the brink of its destruction.... Chastisements will come upon the world.... I feel from what Jesus has said to me, that the time of His Mercy is about to be over. The time of His Justice is about to begin. I feel that the suffering time could be part of the Justice of God. The deeper level of suffering will be the beginning of the Justice of God.'

A Theologian and Prophet on Trials to Come

A small number of theologians have warned about impending dangers. For example, echoing points he had made previously in *Insight*, Bernard Lonergan spoke perceptively in his *Method in Theology* about increasing alienation and the decline of civilisations. Although he wrote in an abstract, objective way, reading between the lines, there is reason to suspect that he thought his analysis applied to contemporary society. He says that instead of responding to impulses that would seek transcendent realities individuals, and indeed whole cultures, can be motivated by egotism. As this happens, the prisons fill with more and more people, men and women who have ignored the law and become involved in selfish crime. When this happens society has to become more lenient in the way in which it interprets the law because there are not enough prison places to accommodate all the potential inmates. In this way, values are watered down, and decline sets in. As he says: 'the law is compromised. It is no longer coincident with justice.'

He goes on to observe in an ominous way: 'A civilisation in decline digs its own grave with a relentless consistency. It cannot be argued out of its self-destructive ways, for argument has a theoretical major premise, theoretical premises are asked to conform to matters of fact, and the facts in the situation produced by decline more and more are the absurdities that proceed from inattention, oversight, unreasonableness and irresponsibility.' Lonergan concludes by stating that a growth in love is the only force that can reverse such an inexorable tendency to decline. 'Self-sacrificing love,' he says, 'will have a redemptive role in human society inasmuch as such love can undo the mischief of decline and restore the cumulative process of progress.'

A prophecy has been widely circulated in the Charismatic Movement. Apparently, it was delivered by Bruce Yocum, a lay theologian, in St Peter's Basilica on Easter Monday 1975. While it speaks of a time of darkness and purification, to come, for the Church, and the world, it goes on to talk about a time of blessing to follow. Here is an approximate translation of paragraphs from an Italian version of the prophecy.

'Since I love you, I want to show you what I am doing in the world today. I want you to be prepared for what is to come. Days of darkness are coming for the world, days of tribulation. Buildings that are firm now, will stand no more. I want you to be prepared my people, so that you will know me. I want you who are faithful to me to know me in a deeper way than you have in the past. I will lead you into the desert. In that hour I will strip you of all that you depend on now so that you will depend only on me.......

'Trials and tribulations will come to you. The consolation that you know now will be removed, but the comfort that you will have is the comfort of my Holy Spirit. I will support you. Come to me. Gather together around me, in close unity. Prepare, since I proclaim a new day, a day of victory and of triumph for your God. It has started already. I will renew my people. I make my people into a unified people. I call upon you to leave the pleasures of the world. I call upon you to renounce worldly desires. I call upon you not to look for the approval of the world. I want to transform your life.'

Surely, these words have been confirmed over the last quarter of a century by events, particularly by the revelation of the clerical abuse of children and subsequent cover-ups by a number of bishops.

A Personal Experience

In the early 1980's I was living in the US. One day while travelling by train to a prayer meeting in Weston School of Theology, in Cambridge, Massachusetts, I felt inwardly that the Lord was saying to me: 'Leave the city with its proud flags and go to the breach in the wall. Go and stand in the breach, the place of insecurity. Stand in the breach where the wind blows, where the jackal cries and where the enemy enters under the cloak of darkness. Stand in the breach and listen to my word. Stand in the breach and pray for yourself and the people. Then call my people to the breach to rebuild the walls of Jerusalem.'

I wasn't sure if these words were from the Lord or not. Following some prayer for help I decided, rightly or wrongly, to cut the bible. If my finger was on the words, 'Rebuild the walls of Jerusalem' I would see them as confirmation of the divine source of my inspiration. I closed my eyes, opened the bible at random. When I looked down and saw that my finger was on verse 18 of psalm 50, which reads, 'rebuild the walls of Jerusalem' I was reassured. I reflected a great deal on that prophetic word and interpreted it in symbolic terms as a call to recognise the diabolic origin of the looming church crisis and to allow myself to share in the vulnerability of the people of God while relying on the word and power of God and interceding for the Church. Although the details of subsequent Church scandals and diminishments shocked and saddened me, the fact that they occurred didn't come as a complete surprise. Finally, I felt that the Lord was calling me to work, with others, in my own small way, for restoration and renewal in the Church.

John Paul's Perspective

Anyone who reads what John Paul II has been writing

over the years will be aware that he has a prophetic perspective on the times in which we live. As early as 1980 he wrote in par. 15 of *The Divine Mercy*: 'If any of our contemporaries do not share the faith and hope that lead me, as a steward of the mysteries of God, to implore God's mercy for humanity in this hour of history, let them at least try to understand the reason for my concern. It is dictated by love for people, for all that is human and which, according to the intuitions of many of our contemporaries, is threatened by an immense danger.' John Paul didn't mention who those contemporaries were. Possibly he had visionaries, prophets or theologians, in mind.

George Weigel points out in his biography of the Pontiff, that John Paul believes that pars 22 and 24 of *The Constitution on the Church In the Modern World* were the theological linchpins of Vatican II. They maintain that we can only know our deepest selves in and through relationship with God in Christ. In par 22 we read: 'It is only in the mystery of the Word made flesh that the mystery of man truly becomes clear.... and all this holds true, not only for Christians but for all people of good will in whose hearts grace is actively present' Par. 24 goes on to draw out the humanistic consequence of this assertion when it adds: 'People can only discover their true selves in a sincere giving of themselves' i.e. through loving relationship expressed in the form of service.

The Pope has reiterated that notion in a number of his writings. Just to give three typical examples.

• In par. 8 of *Veritatis Splendor* (1993) John Paul wrote: 'The man who wishes to understand himself thoroughly…. must so to speak, enter Christ with all his own self; he must 'appropriate' and assimilate the whole of the reality of the Incarnation and Redemption in order to find himself.'

• In par. 25 of *Rosarium Virginis Mariae* (2002) he said: 'Anyone who contemplates Christ through the various stages of his life cannot fail to perceive in him the truth about man. This is the great affirmation of the Second Vatican Council which I have so often discussed in my own teaching since the Encyclical letter *Redemptor Hominis* (1979) : 'it is only in the mystery of the Word made flesh that the mystery of man is seen in its true light.'

• In par. 23 of *Novo Millenio Inuente* (2001), the Pope maintained that contemplating the face of Christ has the effect of 'fully revealing man to man himself.'

Consequences of Theistic Amnesia

However, the Pope warned in par. 38 of *Fides et Ratio* (1999): 'When God is forgotten the creature itself grows unintelligible.'   More recently, he returned to this theme in par 9 of *Ecclesia in Europa* (2003). Having noted that there are obvious signs of hopelessness in Europe, he comments: 'At the root of this loss is an attempt to promote a vision of man apart from God and apart from Christ.' Then he adds: 'This sort of thinking has led to man being considered as the absolute centre of reality, a view which makes him occupy – falsely – the place of God and which forgets that it is not man who creates God, but rather God who creates man. Forgetfulness of God led to the abandonment of man.'

In par. 90 of *Fides et Ratio* (1999) John Paul spoke about some of the likely consequences of this theistic amnesia: 'it makes it possible to erase from the countenance of men and women the marks of their likeness to God and thus leads them little by little either to a destructive will to power or to a solitude without hope.' The destructive will to power, mentioned by John Paul II, is evident in what he refers to as 'the culture of death.' In *Evangelium Vitae* (1995) he pointed out that it can find expression in evils such as abortion, euthanasia and modern warfare.

The solitude without hope he refers to, is quite evident in modern atheism and post-modernism. In par. 9 of *Ecclesia in Europa* he says: 'in this context a vast field has opened up for the unrestrained development of nihilism in philosophy, of relativism in values and morality, and of pragmatism – and even cynical hedonism – in daily life. European culture gives the impression of silent apostasy on the part of people who have all that they need and who live as if God does not exist.' The fact that the proposed constitution of the E.U. doesn't intend to mention either God or the Christian heritage of the continent, seems to confirm this observation. In a sermon delivered on Dec 11th 2003 John Paul said: 'Isn't existential solitude,' he surmised, 'perhaps the profound source of all the dissatisfaction we also perceive in our day? So much insecurity, so many thoughtless reactions originate in our having abandoned God, the rock of our salvation.'

Vulnerability to Evil Influences

In his encyclical, *Dominum Vivifcantem* (1986) Pope John Paul II argued that the agnosticism and atheism that lead to dangerous self-estrangement, is ultimately due to the devil, the father of lies. In par 38 he wrote: 'Satan manages to sow in man's soul the seed of opposition to the one who, from the beginning, would be considered as man's enemy, and not as Father. Man is challenged to become the adversary of God!' Later in the same paragraph he adds: 'through the influence of the father of lies,..... there will be a constant pressure on man to reject God, even to the point of hating him.'

There is reason to suspect that when people are alienated from God and their deepest selves, they are particularly vulnerable to the perverted and perverting activities of the devil who is referred to in scripture as the 'prince of this world' John 12: 31; 14: 30; 16: 11. As He secretly exploits the unacknowledged darkness of the human heart (cf Jeremiah 17: 9) and the unjust structures of society, he seeks to carry out his murderous and dishonest purposes (cf. John 8: 44). As a result, individual people and whole societies can be caught up in enormous splurges of evil such as the violence of the Second Word War and the Holocaust, traumatic economic downturns such as the stock market crash of 1929; and the contemporary plague of HIV aids. As was noted in Chapter 10, Cardinal

Estevez acknowledged this, when he launched the Church's revised rite of exorcism in 1999. In doing so he was echoing the words of scripture: 'For our struggle is not against flesh and blood, but against the rulers, against the authorities, against the powers of this dark world and against the spiritual forces of evil in the heavenly realms' Ephesians 6: 12.

Although historians may describe the causes of tragedies, like those adverted to, in merely human terms, I suspect that in some mysterious way that is beyond the grasp of intellectual understanding, they are ultimately expressions of a pathology of evil that is stirred up by the Evil One. It becomes active to the extent that people ignore God and the divine commandments. In Jungian terms, the devil exploits irrational human complexes and the destructive aspects of the personal and collective shadow to wreak havoc on the world.

The Pope does not believe that God is withdrawing the divine presence from our sinful world, and threatening it with retributive punishment. It is sinful people who are withdrawing from God. In *Crossing the Threshold of Hope*, John Paul has written, 'If God's word is not heard, perhaps it is because 'the ears' of our hearts are not open to it. In this sense Christ spoke about those who 'look but do not see and hear but do not listen or understand' Matthew 13: 13, while the experience of God is always within every person's reach, accessible to him or her in Jesus Christ in the power of the Holy Spirit.... It is truly difficult to speak of the silence of

God. One must speak, rather, of the desire to stifle the voice of God.' As we have already noted, John Paul believes that this lack of receptivity is the ultimate cause of personal and social disorder, of all selfishness and oppression, of violence and revenge. He believes that, if God's presence is temporarily eclipsed and disasters follow; these can in God's providence, have a salutary, purifying effect.

Need for Intercessory Prayer

Speaking about faithful Christians, like himself, the Holy Father said in an address two years ago: 'When every human means seems to fail, believers turn to God..... Even when the Christian feels humanly impotent before the tide of evil, he knows that through prayer he can count on the omnipotence of God who does not abandon those who trust in him. Even if human means fail, hope in God never fails.' In par. 15 of his letter on *The Divine Mercy* he urged: 'Like the prophets, let us appeal to that love which has maternal characteristics and which, like a mother, follows each of her children, each lost sheep, even if they should number millions, even if in the world evil should prevail over goodness.... Let us implore God's mercy for the present generation.'

I got an insight into what this might involve, in the mid 1970's, when I attended an Ecumenical conference hosted by Cardinal Suenens in Malines in Belgium. Towards the end of the proceedings he referred to the fact that in some respects the Church resembled Jerusalem at the time of Nehemiah, the walls of its spirituality have been breached, so that the enemy, in the form of the Trojan Horse of worldliness, can be insinuated into its midst by the Devil, in order to secretly disgorge its malevolent and disruptive influences. Then he opened Isaiah 62: 6-7 and said it was about the need for persistent intercessionary prayer on behalf of the Church. 'I have posted watchmen on your walls, O Jerusalem; they will never be silent day or night. You who call on the Lord, give yourselves no rest, and give him no rest till he establishes Jerusalem and makes her the praise of the earth.'

Need for Evangelisation

For many years now the Pope has thought that there is an urgent need for a Spirit-filled evangelisation of those who are not baptised, or a re-evangelisation of those who, though baptised, live as if Christ did not exist. Numerous people today think they know what Christianity is, yet they do not really know it at all. 'Everywhere,' says the Pope, in par. of *Ecclesia in Europa*, 'a renewed proclamation is needed.' He states in another place: "Rediscover the enthusiasm of proclamation. Hear today... the plea heard at the beginning of the first millennium, when a man of Macedonia appeared in a vision to Paul and begged him: 'Come over to Macedonia and help us!' (Acts 16: 9). Even if it remains unexpressed or even repressed, this is the most profound and genuine plea rising from the hearts of Europeans today, who yearn for a hope which does not disappoint... Let the proclamation of Jesus, which is the Gospel of hope, be your boast and your whole life.'

Happily, there are more and more groups involved in kerygmatic type evangelisation, such as those who conduct RCIA, Alpha, Life in the Spirit Seminars, Philip Retreats, Cursillio courses etc.. If, as a result of efforts like these, the people of our day: 'Seek the Lord while he may be found; and call on him while he is near' Isaiah 55: 6-7, the desolation of the soul, currently being endured by so many in postmodern culture, will eventually come to an end. It could be the prelude to religious revival and future blessing. As the Holy Father said in a prophetic way to a gathering of Christians in Nov 1996: 'God is preparing a great springtime for Christianity, and we can already see its first signs.' However in par. 18, of *Tertio Millennio Adveniente* (1994), John Paul said that such a springtime is not inevitable, it will be revealed: 'if Christians are docile to the action of the Holy Spirit.'

Conclusion

Although the Pope is worried about many negative aspects of our culture, hope predominates. Writing about intimations of better things to come, John Paul pointed out in par. 46 of *Tertio Millennio Adveniente:* 'In society in general, signs of hope include: scientific, technological and especially medical progress in the service of human life, a greater awareness of our responsibility for the environment, efforts to restore peace and justice wherever they have been violated, a desire for reconciliation and solidarity among different peoples, particularly in the complex relationship between the north and the south of the world. In the Church, they include a greater attention to the voice of the Spirit through the acceptance of charisms and the promotion of the laity, a deeper commitment to the cause of Christian unity and the increased interest in dialogue with other religions and with contemporary culture.' In par. 12, of *Ecclesia in Europa*, John Paul points to many more signs of hope in contemporary Europe.

These are not the words of a disenchanted, old man, but a nuanced, balanced and prophetic expression of real fears on the one hand, and a firm and unshakeable Christian hope, on the other. Speaking for myself, I feel more comfortable taking heed of the Holy Father's message, than I do when reading the many messages emanating from visionaries and seers around the world. As he said to religious: 'Those who vigilantly await the fulfilment of Christ's promises are able to bring hope to their brothers and sisters who are often discouraged and pessimistic about the future. Theirs is a hope founded on God's promise contained in the revealed word.' In the meantime, we have reason to have hope for the immediate future.

For example, the prophecy, already adverted to, which was given in St Peter's on Easter Monday 1976 went on to say: 'A time of confusion is coming on the world, but a time of glory is arriving for my church, a time of glory is coming for my people. Once again I will pour out on you all the gifts of my Spirit. I will prepare you for spiritual combat; I will prepare you for a time of evangelisation that the world has never seen. And you won't have anything other than I, but then you will have all: earth, fields, houses, brothers and sisters, love, joy, peace, even more than you had at first.'

More recently, on the 7th February 2003, a Church of Ireland clergyman spoke the following words during a time of intercession in Belfast. In view of their origin, they are as surprising as they are encouraging. Part of the prophetic message reads:

'The Lord has been shaking the Roman Catholic Church. He holds the church in the palm of His hand and he has been shaking it for 20 to 25 years. The church has been rattling around like a nut in a nutshell. All the time the Lord has been shaking it from the outside.

'Now He is going to work on the inside. He throws the church down and cracks it open. A holy and pure church is exposed, what was hidden before can now be seen. As the church, broken, flows out, the Glory of God flows in, like a river of liquid gold.

'This is how The Lord is going to work in the church. Everything in the church that has only been experienced in symbolism and token will now be experienced in full (Ephesians1 : 13-14).

'The candle light – is the Light of Christ,
the incense – is the fragrance of Jesus,
the wafer bread – is the Body of Christ,

the honouring of saints and angels – is holiness and visitations.

'Could it be that symbolism has sustained the church between revivals and kept God's pilot light burning. Soon this generation who have known only symbolism will experience the reality of God (1 Corinthians 13: 12). This will spread through the Catholic Church infrastructure worldwide, producing great love and devotion for the Lord. For the Glory of God to come it will be enough to be associated with the Catholic Church, to go to a Catholic Church or to be called a Catholic, even to have contact with the Catholic Church through occasional ceremonies such as baptism, confirmation, first communion, marriage, funerals. By identifying with the church you will be giving the Lord permission to manifest His glory.'

These words could be a prophetic anticipation of future developments. I hope they are.

Chapter 14

Witnesses to the Supernatural

Consciously or unconsciously, a world-view is a set of assumptions about the basic make up of reality. These presuppositions influence our attitudes, values and beliefs. It is arguable that currently there are three world-views, as far as the supernatural is concerned.

Three Views of the Supernatural

• Firstly, at one end of the spectrum, there is a naturalistic world-view. It denies the existence of the supernatural realm of God, good and evil spirits, heaven, hell, miracles and revelatory religious experiences. Currently, scientist Richard Dawkins is a champion of this atheistic perspective.

• Secondly, at the other end of the spectrum, there is a supernatural Christian world-view that can be traced back to the New Testament in particular. It acknowledges the transcendence of God and the other supernatural realities which are denied by naturalists. Most Pentecostals and Charismatics adopt this faith outlook.

• Thirdly, there is a midway point on the spectrum between a naturalistic and a supernatural point of view. While it accepts basic beliefs such as the existence of God and the prospect of an after-life, it is sceptical about the existence of many other supernatural beliefs, which it dismisses as mere myths. Many liberal Christians espouse this reductionist attitude.

In this chapter I want to suggest that, in our post-modern and secularised world, Christians in general, and members of the Charismatic Movement in particular, are called to be credible witnesses to the reality of the supernatural. Surely, Pope John XXIII had this in mind when he prayed, prior to Vatican II, 'Lord, renew your wonders in our day, as by a new Pentecost,' i.e. in the form of supernatural signs.

A Life Changing Experience

When I was baptised in the Spirit and received a number of the gifts of the Spirit, I moved from my liberal, reductionist world-view, to a more supernatural one. In some ways I resented this trans-formation. I feared that I would be dismissed by many of my well educated colleagues as being intellectually naïve and fundamentalist. Over the years I reassured myself with the thought that believers are called to be fools for Christ's sake (Cf. 1 Corinthians 4: 10).

About twenty years ago I discovered an important key to the supernatural. A number of us were conducting a parish mission in Dublin. I wasn't feeling well at the time. On one of the days I was relieved to find that I was neither appointed preacher or celebrant for that night. However, a few moments before the Eucharist was due to start, I was asked to celebrate the mass. I can recall that when I came forward to say the offertory prayers a profound feeling of powerlessness and emptiness came over me. Placing my hands on the altar, I said a quiet prayer. 'Lord I am at the end of my tether. I am completely drained. I have nothing to offer. How can I lead your people in celebration? Unless you help me, my efforts will be in vain.'

As I began reading the Eucharistic prayer something happened. I became palpably aware of a mysterious Presence. I was so moved by this reassuring experience that, for a brief time, I couldn't speak. During this embarrassing pause I was amazed to find that there was an uncanny silence in the Church. There wasn't a sound. No one was coughing, shuffling or rustling paper. Evidently everyone was aware of the Presence. When I regained my composure, I said, 'I'm sure that you can all sense it. The Holy Spirit has come upon all of us, the Risen Lord is here!' As I continued the mass the anointed sense of Presence deepened. It was one of the most wonderful supernatural experiences of my life.

What a paradox! When I was at my lowest ebb from a human point of view, I was granted one of the greatest blessings of my priestly life. It taught me a number of things. If we are seeking to follow God's will there is no need to be afraid, for we discover that God's 'grace is sufficient for us, for his power is made perfect in weakness.... I can do everything through Him who gives me strength' 2 Corinthians 12: 9; Phillipians 4: 13.

Subsequently, I have referred to experiences like this, as crucifixion points of powerlessness. They are sacred moments of abject inner neediness when we have to depend, absolutely, upon the supernatural power and promises of God. No wonder Jesus advocated a life of material poverty and the central importance of petitionary prayer. For instance, on one occasion he asked the disciples: 'When I sent you without purse, bag or sandals, did you lack anything?' Luke 22: 35. As long as we prayerfully depend upon the providence and provision of God, even to the point of healings and miracles, we modern day disciples, like those in the New Testament, will lack nothing.

Power in Powerlessness

Nowadays when I face crucifixion points of powerlessness, instead of anxiously wrestling with my fears, I try nestling in the Lord through faith. Here are a few examples:

• I am trying to overcome an addiction, a sinful habit e.g. a longstanding resentment, which, despite my own best efforts, still defeats me.

- A person I care about has a serious spiritual problem, e.g. a loss of faith, or an adulterous relationship. From a human point of view there is nothing I can do to help.
- I am asked to pray for a relative or friend who has an illness like the flu, or an incurable disease such as cancer or multiple sclerosis.
- I am asked to pray for a person who wants to be baptised in the Spirit, or to experience inner healing.
- I am called to help people who are frightened by the fact that their house seems to be haunted by a poltergeist.

Whenever we are faced with situations like these, we are being invited to rely on God's supernatural help in accordance with whatever scripture promises seem relevant. To this end, we can ask God to guide our prayers, if necessary, by a prophetic word of knowledge.

Conclusion

As a result of secularisation the sense of the supernatural has been dying in the lives of many people. We have a choice to make. Firstly, if a week goes by, and we have not exercised expectant faith, we may be allowing ourselves, implicitly at least, to slip back into a liberal or even a naturalistic world-view. Secondly, while those who do not espouse a supernatural world-view will not be persuaded of its existence by force of mere rational arguments, they may change their minds if they experience the supernatural in action, e.g. in the form of answered

prayer or deeds of power.   As Pope Paul said in par.
41 of *Evangelisation Today*: 'The people of our day are
more impressed by witness than teachers, and if they
listen to teachers it is because they also bear witness'

Chapter 15

Charismatics and Christian

Maturity

Hebrews 5: 12-14 implies that there are two main stages in the Christian life, a childish, beginners stage, and a more mature, adult one. The inspired author writes: 'You need milk, not solid food! Anyone who lives on milk, being still an infant, is not acquainted with the teaching about righteousness. But solid food is for the mature.' In par. 72 of *Catechesis in our Time*, Pope John Paul II seemed to echo these words when he wrote: 'Renewal in the Spirit will be authentic and will have great fruitfulness in the Church, not so much according as it gives rise to extraordinary charisms, (i.e. milk) but according as it leads the greatest possible number of the faithful, as they travel their daily paths, to make a humble, patient and persevering effort to know the mystery of Christ better and better, and to bear witness to it. (i.e. solid food)'

Two Baptisms

Jesus experienced two baptisms. There was his 'baptism in the Spirit' at the Jordan. It inaugurated his public ministry and empowered him to proclaim and demonstrate the unconditional love of God in an anointed way. This was obvious when Jesus ministered in his native Galilee. He performed numerous healings and miracles, attracted large crowds and seemed to be very successful. However, Jesus also talked about a second baptism, one which would immerse him in suffering. He said: 'I have a baptism with which to be baptised, and what stress I am under until it is completed!' Luke 12: 49. It reached its climax in holy week when success gave way to failure, adulation gave way to hostility, and charismatic activity gave way to apparent powerlessness. For example, when he was hanging on the cross the scorners cried out in Matthew 27: 42: 'He saved others; he cannot save himself. If he is the king of Israel; let him come down from the cross now, and we will believe in him.' But nothing miraculous happened. Instead the ever faithful Jesus felt abandoned by God and man, and in this state he died.

At this point a question arises. Which baptism did most to inaugurate the coming of the Kingdom? Obviously both did. But surely the suffering and death of Jesus did more than his healings and miracles to bear testimony to God's love. As St Paul said: 'God proves his love for us in that while we still were sinners Christ died for us.... For Jews demand signs and Greeks desire wisdom, but we proclaim Christ crucified, a stumbling block to Jews and foolishness to Gentiles, but to those who are called, both Jews and Greeks, Christ the power of God and the wisdom of God' Romans 5: 8; 1 Corinthians 1: 22-24.

It seems to me that charismatic prayer groups are very good at helping people to accept the first baptism and its charismatic implications. They are not so good at helping people to accept the second and its spiritual and practical implications. As Tom Smail, a leader in the Protestant Charismatic Renewal once observed: 'A need centered renewal is hampered and hindered because many involved in it have not been converted from need to obedience, from satisfying themselves to being at God's disposal.' Perhaps that's why so many prayer groups seem to be losing their sense of vitality and direction.

Two Stages of Spiritual Growth

I can recall an eminent spiritual director saying once: 'charismatic prayer groups are good at getting their members established in new life in the Spirit, but they seem to be at a loss when it comes to helping people to grow and mature.' When I heard him make this observation, I felt that it was very perceptive. In his *Exercises*, St Ignatius describes two stages of Christian growth:

111

In the first, e.g. the period after baptism in the Spirit, the main dynamic at work is that the person is motivated by a self-centered need to receive the mercy, love, consolations and gifts of God. I may say in passing that there is nothing wrong with this kind of desire; it's prompted by the Lord and is a necessary preparation for the second stage of spiritual development. A problem arises when charismatic individuals and groups get stuck at this stage for one reason or another, and fail to move on to the second.

In the second stage, the main dynamic at work in the person is motivated by a God-centered desire to be united to Jesus, poor humble and dependant on God. The person no longer focuses on the gifts or consolations of God, but rather on the God of consolation and the gifts. Inwardly, the person shifts from asking, 'what can God do for me?' to 'what can I do for God?' More often than not the person at this stage wants to be 'guided by the Spirit' (Galations 5: 16; 18; 25). A number of scripture scholars agree that this is the key to Pauline ethics. The Christian life is not a list of do's and don'ts. It is the gift of being moved by the Spirit of God, and the key to life is to allow the Spirit to lead. A crucial point: when confronted with any moral decision, great or small, the Christian's first question should be, where does the Spirit lead me in this?

The Social Justice Dimension of Renewal

As far back as 1971, the Synod of Bishops stated quite

correctly that justice is an essential aspect of the preaching of the gospel. However many charismatic groups and individuals have neglected this dimension. Perhaps this is due to three main reasons. Firstly, many charismatics share a questionable view that the world is corrupt and that Christians should not get involved in it, lest they become contaminated. Secondly, many charismatics are so preoccupied with building community and personal renewal that they have often neglected justice issues. It has been said, with some justification, that some charismatics are so heavenly minded as to be of no earthy use. Thirdly, when they think of evangelisation, many charismatics see it exclusively in terms of preaching the Good News, e.g. by means of Life in the Spirit Seminars and Alpha courses. If and when charismatics do get involved in the search for fair, humane treatment for the disadvantaged members of society, their most common understanding of social action is that of doing works of mercy on an individual basis. However, they often neglect to identify and change the unjust structures that produce human oppression in the first place. Charismatics could learn from the Vincent de Paul Society and others who commission research into the causes of injustice and who make regular submissions to governmental and local authorities recommending remedial action.

Conclusion

The leaders of Charismatic groups need to encourage their members, by means of good teaching and example, to move beyond a fixation with their own needs to focus on the will of God and the needs of their neighbour. Otherwise they will become 'holy huddles,' turned in on themselves. In so far as Charismatic groups do this, they will continue to lose some of their best members. They will become disillusioned and go elsewhere in search of on-going spiritual growth. Diocesan and national service committees have a responsibility to work out the implications of these points for the renewal and to do something practical about them.

Chapter 16

Charisms and the New Evangelisation

Following his baptism at the Jordan, Jesus did two main things. Acts 1:1 says he began to do and to teach. In other words he proclaimed the Good News of God's love, especially to the poor, and he actively demonstrated the reality of that Good News in two main ways.

Firstly, he related to the people in a compassionate, understanding way which was devoid of judgement or condemnation. He did not dominate them. Instead he came as one who serves. He responded in a humble way to their deepest needs. He longed for their liberation, not only from spiritual bondage but also from the unjust structures of society.

Secondly, he performed deeds of power such as healings, exorcisms and miracles. These signs and wonders were not intended to prove that what Jesus said was true. Rather they were the Good News in action, a concrete expression of God's offer of unconditional mercy and love to those who trusted in the Lord. It is interesting to recall that when St John the Baptist was in prison he sent messengers to ask Jesus whether he was the promised messiah. Jesus pointed to his proclamation and demonstration of the Good News when he replied: 'Go back and report to John what you hear and see: The blind receive sight, the lame walk, those who have leprosy are cured, the deaf hear, the dead are raised, and the good news is preached to the poor' Matthew 11: 4-5.

The Commission to Proclaim and Demonstrate the Good News

During his lifetime Jesus instructed the apostles to do the same. Like him, they were to proclaim and demonstrate the coming of the Kingdom of God. For example in Luke 9: 1-2 we read: 'And he called the twelve together and gave them power and authority over all demons and to cure diseases, and he sent them out to preach the kingdom of God and to heal.' Before his ascension into heaven, the Lord commissioned the apostles to continue to do the same in the future. In Mark 16: 15-19 we read: 'He said to them, 'Go into all the world and preach the good news to all creation. Whoever believes and is baptised will be saved, but whoever does not believe will be condemned. And these signs will accompany those who believe: In my name they will drive out demons; they will speak in new tongues; they will pick up snakes with their hands; and when they drink deadly poison, it will not hurt them at all; they will place their hands on sick people, and they will get well.' There is clear evidence in the Acts and especially the earlier epistles of Paul, that the apostles did carry out the Lord's instructions. They not only proclaimed the good news, they demonstrated it in deeds of power. As Acts 2: 43 testifies, 'Many wonders and signs were done through the apostles.'

There is clear evidence that the charisms were exercised in the early years of Christianity. For example in the 4th century St Hilary wrote in a commentary on Psalm 64: 'We who are reborn through the sacrament of baptism have the greatest joy, as we perceive within us the first stirrings of the Holy Spirit, as we begin to understand mysteries; we gain full knowledge of prophecy, speech full of wisdom, security in our hope, gifts of healing and dominion over devils who are made subject to us. These gifts like drops of liquid permeate our inner self, and so beginning, little by little they produce fruits in abundance.' It is equally clear that a few centuries later the charisms had all but faded away. Why this happened, is not entirely clear. There were a number of possible reasons.

- Firstly, there was what sociologist Emile

Durkheim referred to as the ritualisation of charism. In other words the Church relied on official ministries and the administration of the sacraments as means of grace.

• Secondly, there was a struggle between the institutional and 'charismatic' wings of Christianity. For example, at the end of the second century the Montanists, who were charismatic, were finally condemned as heretics. As a result charisms and charismatics were no longer trusted.

• Thirdly, Medieval theology, from the time of Pope St Gregory the Great (540-604) was, by and large, unsympathetic to the notion of pre-rational forms of religious experience such as tongues and healings. In the high Middle Ages this tendency was reinforced by St Thomas Aquinas (1225-1274) and some centuries later by the rationalistic world view of the Enlightenment.

As a result, the charismatic dimension of Christian life was overlooked in favour of the doctrinal and ministerial authority of the institutional Church. Priests and people expected the Spirit to be manifested by the witness of lives well lived, merciful deeds, and in action for justice; but not by unusual charismatic activity. St Thomas Aquinas taught that canonisable saints were the only exception to this rule during their lifetimes and after their deaths. He wrote: 'True miracles cannot be wrought save by the power of God, because God works them....... in proof of a person's holiness which God desires to propose as an example of virtue.'

Charismatic Revival at Vatican II

For Catholics, all this began to change at the Second Vatican Council. In par 12 of the *Constitution on the Church* and par 3 of the *Constitution on the Laity*, the pope and bishops made ten important points to do with the more unusual charisms.

1. Grace comes to us primarily through sacraments and clerical ministry.
2. Grace also comes through the gifts of the Spirit in general, and the charisms mentioned in 1 Corinthians 12: 8-10 in particular.
3. The Holy Spirit distributes what are variously referred to as simple and exceptional gifts, among lay people.
4. These gifts are given to build up the Church in holiness and to develop people.
5. The charisms are a wonderful means of apostolic vitality.
6. These gifts are to be received with gratitude and consolation.
7. Lay people have a right to exercise their charisms and ministries. This right comes from their baptism and not from the clergy.
8. Lay people have a duty to use their charisms for the good of the Church and the world.
9. Bishops and clergy should test the charisms to see that they are genuine and used for the common good.
10. However, the clergy should be careful not to quench the Spirit by an arbitrary use of authority.

Classification of the Charisms

Paul's theology of the gifts is an expression of his experience, not of his reading. So when he listed the charisms in 1 Corinthians 12: 8-10, he probably did so in the light of his personal experience. I would suggest that they can be classified in the following way:

• There are charisms of revelation that enable the believer to know the presence, word and will of the Lord.

• There are charisms of proclamation that enable the believer to preach, teach or share the Good News.

• There are charisms of demonstration which manifest the Good news e.g. by means of liberating deeds of power.

This is a quasi-sacramental view, where word and deed, together conspire to make the risen Christ present. As St Paul once observed: 'For the kingdom of God is not a matter of (mere) talk but of power' 1 Corinthians 4: 20.

Charisms and Proclaiming the Good News

I'm convinced that evangelisation does not have to involve a choice between traditional and charismatic approaches, what is sometimes referred to as presence and power evangelism. Nowadays many evangelists aim to demonstrate the truth of the gospel proclamation, not just by the witness of transformed lives, charitable deeds, and action for justice but also by the performance of 'signs and wonders' such as healings, exorcisms and occasional miracles. It could be added, in the light of the Pauline theology of ministry, that those who evangelise are more likely to receive the charisms of power than others.

Francis MacNutt had the ministry of evangelisation in mind when, in 1979, he wrote in an article in *New Covenant* magazine: 'A gift of preaching is strengthened by other manifestations of the power of the Holy Spirit. St Paul states that in his sermons he did not depend on arguments that belonged to philosophy but on a 'demonstration of the Spirit and power' 1 Corinthians 2: 4. St Thomas Aquinas, in his commentary on this passage, states that the preacher of the gospel should preach as Jesus did, confirming the message either through healings and miracles or by living such a holy life that can only be explained by the power of the Spirit. If I preach the power of Jesus Christ to save and redeem the whole person, people want to see that power made real. They want to see the saving, freeing power of Jesus when we pray that the spiritually sick be given the power to repent, and that the emotionally and physically sick be healed, and may be made better as a sign that the messages of salvation and healing are true.'

Conclusion

Pope Paul the VI seemed to endorse this point of view when he spoke at the official launch of Cardinal Suenens' influential book, *A New Pentecost?* In the course of his address he departed from his prepared text to say these spontaneous words: 'How wonderful it would be if the Lord would again pour out the charisms in increased abundance, in order to make the Church fruitful, beautiful and marvellous, and to enable it to win the attention and astonishment of the profane and secularised world.' There is evidence, which indicates that in recent years the charisms mentioned in 1 Corinthians 12: 8-10 have indeed been given to men and women in all the Christian denominations. By and large, Pentecostals and Charismatic groups who evangelise by proclaiming the good news with accompanying charisms such as healing, have been growing fast, while those who do not, have tended to decline.

While the Magisterium of the Church appreciates the importance and role of the charisms, it sees them as a means to an end. For example, par. 2003 of the *Catechism of the Catholic Church*, says: 'Whatever their character - sometimes it is extraordinary, such as the gift of miracles or of tongues - charisms are oriented toward sanctifying grace, and are for the common good of the church. They are at the service of charity which builds up the church.' Finally, as noted in Chapter 1, Pope John Paul offered a word of caution in his encyclical *Catechesis in Our time*. He pointed out that the Charismatic Renewal should not be evaluated on the basis of its charismatic activity but rather, for its ability to lead the greatest possible number of the faithful to make a humble, patient and persevering effort to know the mystery of Christ and to bear witness to it.

Chapter 17

Charisms and Ecumenism

It is has been said that we are living in the post-modern age. Nowadays many people suspect that there is no such thing as absolute doctrinal or moral truth.   What impresses them, therefore, are not ideological beliefs but genuine experiences.   As Pope John Paul II himself acknowledged, 'People today are more impressed by experience than by doctrine.'   The great thing about the Spirit and the gifts of the Spirit, is the fact that they are so experiential.   When people both within and without the different churches see them in action, especially the gifts of healing and deliverance, they are inclined to break down barriers, and to challenge traditional prejudices.   While we usually think of witness winning over non-believers to faith, witness by means of charismatic activity, can also win over members of other churches who, for one reason or another, are either mistrustful or antagonistic. That was the way in my own life. As a young priest, the truth of the gospel of love hadn't fallen from my head to my heart. One effect of this lack of charity, was the fact that I was prejudiced against Protestants. When I was 29 I went to a week-end retreat. The talks were given by a Church of Ireland minister. His anointed words really moved me. At one point I spoke to him and he offered to pray for me. Although I was a little reluctant to be prayed with by a non-Catholic, I said 'yes.' Having read a passage from Ephesians 3: 14-20 he laid hands on me and prayed that I might receive an outpouring of the Spirit and his gifts. I immediately experienced a spiritual awakening. I became consciously aware of God's unconditional love for me and began to pray profusely in tongues. As a result of this religious illumination, I was fully persuaded that the Lord was strongly at work in members of other churches. This was confirmed the morning after my baptism in the Spirit. I was praying with a number of Catholics and Protestants. It was a bright Spring day. The light was streaming through the windows. When I saw its dappled textures reflected on the faces of the people, I thought that they were like so many coloured pieces in a large mosaic. I sensed that their differing gifts, graces and charisms were revealing the presence of the risen Jesus to me. There was Jesus the healer in one, Jesus the prophet in another…. etc.

That primordial awareness of our unity in the Spirit of God has never left me. Happily, during the last century, the charisms have been poured out in all denominations. The community of believers, whatever churches they belong to, are empowered for service by the gifts listed by Paul in 1 Corinthians 12: 8-10, Romans 12: 6-9; and Ephesians 4: 7-14. They are rooted in love, express love and are intended to build up that same love among Christians. Whereas our differing beliefs can sometimes be the cause of acrimony and division, the gifts tend to unite. Through their common exercise, Christians are drawn closer to Jesus and therefore to one another.

I have found that the charisms have a unique ability to build bridges of understanding and unity. For instance, many years ago I took charge of a parish in Gibraltar while the priest was away on holiday. About a mile away there was a very active Pentecostal church. It had attracted quite a number of lapsed Catholics. The pastor used to tell his congregation that R.C.s were not saved because they hadn't been born again through personal faith in Christ. However, many of the Pentecostals were disconcerted when they heard that a Catholic priest in a nearby parish seemed to have been baptised in the Spirit and could pray in tongues. At one point a deputation came to chat and pray with me. I suspect that they wanted to see for themselves whether the rumours were true. When they saw that I had indeed been baptised in the Spirit and exercised the gifts of the Spirit, they were persuaded that I, like many other Catholics, had truly been saved. As a result a number of the lapsed Catholics, returned to the Church while the attitude of the other Pentecostals was challenged and changed. They had been won over, not by doctrinal arguments, but rather by the exercise of the charisms. They interpreted them as a sure sign of the Spirit's activity. As St Paul testified: 'My speech and my message were not in plausible words of wisdom, but in demonstration of the Spirit and of power....The kingdom of God does not consist in talk but in power' 1 Corinthians 2: 4; 1 Corinthians 4: 20.

It was much the same on the home front. I can recall an occasion when a number of Catholics and Protestants were invited to conduct a day of renewal in Coleraine. David McKee, a Presbyterian minister, gave the talks. Afterwards he asked a Catholic lay man, an Anglican vicar, and myself to join him in praying for people. As we did so, many of them, Catholics and Protestants alike, began to fall to the ground under the power of the Spirit. When the meeting was over, David called me aside. 'That is the first time I have ever seen people resting in the Spirit' he said, 'why do you think it has happened today?' 'As far as I'm concerned,' I replied, 'There can be only one answer. God is honouring our united witness by blessing our ministry in a special way. As Psalm 133: says: 'How good and delightful it is to live together as brothers and sisters...for there Yahweh bestows a blessing.'

In an article entitled, *'Ecumenical Origins of the Charismatic Renewal,'* Peter Hocken has made the important observation that the Charismatic movement is the only renewal movement in the Catholic Church to have had its origin in Protestantism. Not only that, renewal in the Spirit and reconciliation between churches have been virtually synonymous in Charismatic Renewal. I'm also persuaded that it is only in the light of shared experiences, such as the ones I have described, that we will be enabled to reconcile our doctrinal differences in such a way as to bring about ecclesial convergence. So, I'm utterly convinced that the gifts have an indispensable ecumenical role to play.

Chapter 18

Apostasy and Hope

A few years ago it began to dawn upon me that we Catholics are living in a time of mass apostasy. The word is derived from Greek, meaning 'to depart', i.e. from Christianity, either voluntarily or as a result of compulsion. In the Bible the word was used to signify 'abandonment of belief' and 'infidelity to Yahweh.' There seems to be a grey area between the notions of apostasy and lapsation. Many Catholics abandon Christian practices such as church going, prayer and New Testament ethics, without necessarily abandoning Christian beliefs. One way or the other, however, it amounts to desertion on a mass scale. It could be argued that in our culture apostasy takes two forms. Firstly, there are those Catholics who were baptised, confirmed and brought up as Christians. Many of them were sacramentalised, but never fully evangelised. As a result, in Gordon Allport's sense, their faith was extrinsic rather than intrinsic. So, when they turn their backs on their religion it could be said that they were abandoning a faith they had never really made their own. Sadly, there are also those who were once committed christians but who, for one reason or another, have turned their backs on Christ and his teaching.

In Western Europe there are millions of baptised people who seem to have abandoned Christian beliefs and practices for the reasons described. The evidence is pretty obvious. Only a small minority attend church on a regular basis; Christian ethics, especially where human sexuality and business are concerned, are largely ignored. Seminaries are emptying and religious orders are dying. As a regular visitor to book shops, I have noticed that the sections devoted to specifically Christian literature are shrinking, while those devoted to self-help, New Age books, and other forms of esoteric belief are growing. Nowadays it is not uncommon to hear public figures saying that we are living in a post-Catholic, post-Christian era.   The media in a number of countries either ignore Christian subjects or repeatedly engage in disparaging comments that dismiss Christianity as an anachronism.   It is significant that the proposed European constitution contains no reference to God. As was noted in Chapter 13, Pope John Paul has observed: 'European culture gives the impression of silent apostasy on the part of people who have all that they need and who live as if God did not exist.'

Apostasy in the Early Church

Apostasy was a recurring problem in the Old Testament. For example, when Moses discovered that the people had abandoned the Lord and worshipped the golden calf, the Lord said to him: 'Go down now, because your people who you brought out of Egypt have apostasised.' Exodus 32:7. Apostasy was also a problem in the early Church. Some people turned their backs on the faith during the Roman persecutions, others were bewitched by other belief systems such as Gnosticism. Therefore it is not surprising to find that the New Testament warned against the dangers of apostasy. For example, St. Paul said that many people rejected the gospel message because their understanding was darkened by Satan. He said: 'the god of this world has blinded the minds of the unbelievers, to keep them from seeing the light of the gospel of the glory of Christ' 2 Corinthians 4: 4. Others abandoned the faith as a result of false teaching. As Jesus had warned: 'Many false prophets will arise and lead many astray' Matthew 24: 11. In another place we are told that there was little hope for those who, having once known the Lord, had turned their backs on him. 'It is impossible to restore again to repentance those who have once been enlightened, and have tasted the heavenly gift, and have shared in the Holy Spirit, and have tasted the goodness of the word of God and the powers of the age to come, and then have fallen away, since on their own they are crucifying again the Son of God and are holding him up to contempt.' Hebrews 6: 4-6. In another place Paul referred to the apostasy that would precede the second coming. He wrote: 'The Spirit clearly says that in later times some will abandon the faith and follow deceiving spirits and things taught by demons. Man will oppose and will exalt himself over everything that is called God or is worshiped, so that he sets himself up in God's temple, proclaiming himself to be God.' 1 Timothy 4: 1; 2 Thessalonians 2: 3-4.

Apostolic Apostasy and Renewal of Faith

Recently, it occurred to me that there is a surprising and instructive account of apostolic apostasy in the gospel of John. We read: 'Simon Peter, Thomas, Nathanael from Cana in Galilee, the sons of Zebedee, and the two other disciples were together. 'I'm going out to fish,' Simon Peter told them, and they said, 'We'll go with you.' So they went out and got into the boat, but that night they caught nothing' John 21: 2-3.

To appreciate what was involved, we need to remember that, not only had Peter and the apostles accompanied Jesus throughout his public ministry, he had also appeared to them following his death and resurrection. We are told that: 'He breathed on them and said, 'Receive the Holy Spirit. If you forgive anyone his sins, they are forgiven; if you do not forgive them, they are not forgiven'' John 20: 22-23. In spite of all this, Peter and his companions returned to their old way of life. In his authoritative commentary on John's gospel, John Marsh surmises that: 'It may well have appeared that now the Passover time was over, and Jesus dead, even though he had appeared to them in Jerusalem, the only thing left now that they were back in Galilee was to resume their normal tasks.'

Marsh adds: 'It is precisely in doing a 'secular ' job, even at a time of desertion and apostasy, that the glorified Lord will make himself known.' What is so reassuring about John's account of this incident is the fact that, rather than rejecting them, or engaging in angry recrimination, Jesus responded to Peter and the apostles in a gentle and helpful way. He told them where to cast their net, invited them to share breakfast with him, and went on to commission Peter to feed his sheep. In other words, Jesus not only appeared to the apostles in the midst of their apostasy, he authorised and empowered them to be faithful fishers of men by means of evangelisation. It was as if Jesus were saying to them that they should learn from their apostasy; God's power would be made perfect in the very weakness that was evident in their infidelity. They would be effective in their mission as long as they relied on Him, rather than themselves.

Hope for the Future

We face similar challenges in the 21st century. Many contemporary Europeans, including catholics in Britain and Ireland, may have turned their backs on God, but I'm quite sure that God's back will not be turned on them. God will not punish them either. But they will be allowed to suffer the inevitable consequences of alienation from God, such as a time of desolation of spirit and inner turmoil, which may also find expression in social upheaval and even violence. God will use these inner and outer tribulations to bring about mature disillusionment and purification. That may lead many people to be secretly, if not openly, receptive to divine revelation. Then Jesus could, unexpectedly, manifest himself to the people of Europe, as he did to the apostles, while calling and empowering them to be faithful to their Christian heritage.

In his letter on the Church in Europe, Pope John Paul II addresses this appeal to the people of the continent: '*Europe*, as you stand at the beginning of the third millennium, 'Open the doors to Christ! Be yourself. Rediscover your origins. Relive your roots.' Down the centuries you have received the treasure of Christian faith. It has grounded your life as a society on principles drawn from the Gospel, and traces of this are evident in the art, literature, thought and culture of your nations. But this heritage does not belong just to the past; it is a project in the making, to be passed on to future generations, for it has indelibly marked the life of the individuals and peoples who together have forged the continent of Europe' (Par 120). Later in the same letter he says, 'Do not be afraid! The Gospel is not against you, but for you .... Be confident! In the Gospel, which is Jesus, you will find the sure and lasting hope to which you aspire .... Be certain! The Gospel of hope does not disappoint!' (Par. 121) Hopefully, large numbers of people in Europe will respond to this call in the future as a result of a new and effective evangelisation that leads to revival and renewal in the Holy Spirit.

Conclusion

In the meantime, those of us who by the grace of God continue to acknowledge God's sovereignty in our lives, can do a number of constructive things. Firstly, we should grieve for people's forgetfulness of God. We can listen to these plaintiff words: 'The Lord has a case against his people; he is lodging a charge against Israel (Europe). 'My people, what have I done to you? How have I burdened you? Answer me' Micah 6: 2-3. Secondly, this sense of mourning can find positive expression in fervent prayers for the grace of Christian revival in Europe, and the new Springtime predicted by Pope John Paul. They can be expressed in words like these: 'O Lord, I have heard of your renown, and I stand in awe, O Lord, of your work. In our own time revive it; in our own time make it known' Habakuk 3: 2. Thirdly, we can create informal Christian networks, while offering one another mutual support, encouragement and good example. Fourthly, we need to be attentive to genuine prophetic messages, such as those mentioned in chapters fourteen and fifteen, which give us intimations of what on earth the Lord is about to do for heaven's sake. Fifthly we need to continue to explore new ways of evangelising, or re-evangelising those who have forgotten God. Sixthly, we can pray, in this age of apostasy, that we ourselves will be granted the grace of uncompromising fidelity and final perseverance.

Chapter 19

Charismatics and
Contemporary Ethics

The book of Judges describes what happened after the death of Joshua and before the establishment of the Jewish monarchy. Chapter Two points out that there was a tendency towards infidelity among the people. 'Abandoning the Lord, the God of their fathers, ...they followed the other gods of the various nations around them.' For example, Judges 17: 1-7, tells us that when Micah returned stolen silver to his mother she had it melted down and made into an idol. There was also moral decline. For example, in Judges 19: 22-29 we are told how, in order to protect himself, a Levite gave his concubine to a group of debauched men who had originally intended to sexually assault him. Instead, they savagely raped her over and over again. Shortly, after her terrible ordeal she died. The last verse of the book, encapsulates the basic reason for such a widespread breakdown of faith and morals: 'There was no king in Israel; everyone did what was right in his own eyes' Judges 21: 25.

It has struck me on a number of occasions that this verse has considerable relevance in contemporary Britain and Ireland where, in Yeats' words, it often seems that: 'Things fall apart; the centre cannot hold; ....the best lack all conviction.' Like other Western societies, ours are postmodern, and secular. They maintain that, rather than being an objective fact, all our knowledge - including moral knowledge - is at best partial and provisional. Nothing is absolutely certain. As a result there is a growing tendency to make ethics a matter of private opinion. There is considerable evidence to show how many people, in public and private life, have been rewriting the commandments to suit themselves.

Over the past 20 years, three pan-European surveys have indicated how many men and women in these islands adopt an 'a la carte' approach to morality by picking and choosing what seems right to them. They do so in the name of personal conscience, believing that there aren't any reliable, objective standards, for judging right from wrong. For example, a well known pop singer reflected the views of many when he confessed in the Sunday Independent, May 12th 2002: 'I have my faith, I don't go to church now or have a priest dictate how to live my life. I read the Bible and do things my own way.' This privatisation of morality is evident in society in general. In recent years there has been a significant increase in the numbers having intercourse before marriage, living together as partners, using artificial forms of contraception, engaging in gay sex, having abortions etc. Others advocate practices such as euthanasia, artificial insemination and the cloning of individuals. Their theme tune could be Frank Sinatra's, 'I did it my way!'

I believe that, within the present context, Pope John Paul II's teaching is prophetic. He maintains that humanity 'is threatened by an immense danger.' When he wrote *Splendour of the Truth* (1993), he was stating that we need to restore our reverence for God's authority as the heavenly King. The Lord has revealed the moral precepts which are reliably taught by the Church. In our search for ethical guidelines we should make use of our reason, as illumined by divine truth. Together they tell us that there are acts, such as euthanasia, child sex abuse, torture, rape, injustice, pornography and genocide which are always intrinsically wrong. Intentions, circumstances or consequences can never make them right.

During his visit to Ireland in 1979, the Pope warned Irish people, and by extension all Catholics in the Western world, that they are involved in a tremendous religious and ethical struggle. He stated in a prescient way: 'Your country seems in a sense to be living again the temptations of Christ: You are being asked to prefer the kingdoms of the world and their splendour to the kingdom of God. Satan the tempter, the adversary of Christ, will use all his might and all his deceptions to win you for the way of the world. What a victory he would gain, what a blow he would inflict on the body of Christ in the world if he could seduce men and women away from Christ. Now is the time of testing. This generation is once more a generation of decision.' Surely, the infidelities, scandals and defections of recent years are proof positive that, sadly, these words have been fulfilled in the lives of many.

What should people in the Charismatic Renewal do in order to redress this situation? I think there are three priorities. Firstly, we need to intercede for those who are torn between the beliefs and values of the world and those of the gospel. As Pope John Paul said in Limerick in 1979: 'Dear sons and daughters...., pray, pray not to be led into temptation.... I ask you today for a great, intense and growing prayer for all the people, ... for all the Church .... Pray that you will not fail in the test. Pray as Jesus taught us to pray: 'Lead us not into temptation'.'

Secondly, we need to help fellow Catholics, who are sacramentalised but not truly evangelised, to make a wholehearted personal commitment to Jesus Christ as their Lord and Saviour. Otherwise, even if they have a desire to carry the yoke of New Testament morality, it will prove to be too heavy a burden for those who haven't yet experienced the liberating power of the Good News. As a result, they will suffer from understandable feelings of failure and condemnation, and walk away from the Church. Surely this is what often happens, especially in poorer city areas. This dynamic can only be reversed by means of such things as personal witness, Life in the Spirit Seminars, Alpha Courses, Cursillio Weekends, CaFE, RCIA, coupled with a radical critique and reform of the unjust structures of society. It is only when growing numbers of people experience a consequent spiritual awakening that the Spirit will lead them to have both the conscientious desire and the inner power to accept and live by the revealed truths taught by the Church.

Thirdly, when people have become true disciples of Christ, we need to inform them that in spite of what secular, postmodern culture maintains, there are objective, unchanging ethical guidelines to live by. We need to teach these truths with confidence, in the firm belief that, although they are hard to carry out, they are a reliable guide to true Christian freedom, and holiness. Wouldn't it be great, in the years to come, if, as a result of intercession, effective evangelisation and good moral teaching, we experienced such Christian revival and renewal in our two islands, that we could say: 'In these days, Christ is King, and everyone does what is right in God's eyes.'

Chapter 20

Overcoming Feelings of Injustice and Hurt

Many years ago I heard someone say that justice is a matter of giving people what they are due in accordance with their human dignity and rights. When children are brought into the world by their parents, they deserve to have their physical, emotional and spiritual needs met in a reasonable way. When carers fail to meet these needs for one reason or another, there is not only a feeling of deprivation and hurt, but also one of injustice. This reflection will focus on one of the liberating ways in which Christians can respond to the injustices they may have suffered in childhood and afterwards.

The Bernardo's children's charity, has a striking slogan,

'childhood lasts a lifetime.' In many ways it is true. It echoes the traditional view that, 'the child is father to the man.' In an 1914 essay entitled *Some Reflections on a Schoolboy Psychology* Sigmund Freud said to former classmates and teachers at his alma mater: 'Psychoanalysis has taught us that the individual's emotional attitudes to other people, which are of extreme importance to his later behaviour are already established at an unexpectedly early age. The nature and quality of the human child's relations to people of his own and the opposite sex have already been laid down in the first six years of his life.' There is a well known quote which puts this in simple terms:

If a child lives with criticism, he learns to condemn.
If a child lives with hostility, he learns to fight.
If a child lives with ridicule, he learns to be shy.
If a child lives with shame, he learns to feel guilty.
If a child lives with tolerance, he learns to be patient.
If a child lives with encouragement, he learns
 confidence.
If a child lives with praise, he learns to appreciate.
If a child lives with security, he learns to have faith.
If a child lives with approval, he learns to like himself.
If a child lives with acceptance and friendship,
he learns to find love in the world.

Many children limp out of childhood as a result of lacking the unconditional love that they needed. More often than not, it is usually due to the inadequacies of parents and carers rather than their malice. One way or the other, deficits in the experience of empathic and reliable caring leads to subsequent feelings of anxiety, low self-esteem and mistrust. Some children are the victims of abuse. A minority experience physical abuse e.g. savage beatings; about one in five children is abused sexually; others are abused emotionally e.g. due to constant put-downs; while others are abused spiritually e.g. when adults try to control their behaviour by teaching them to fear God as a harsh and punitive judge.

Recently, it has occurred to me that if parents have been on the receiving end of abuse and trauma in childhood; and if they are unable to acknowledge and resolve their feelings, they will leak out from the unconscious in the form of unhealthy attitudes and behaviours. Not only that, their children seem to absorb their emotional pain by a principal of osmosis. What confuses them in adult life is the fact that there are not adequate or proportionate explanations for their inner pain in their own childhood experiences. As scripture suggests, the inadequacies of the parents are visited on their children and grand children (Cf. Deuteronomy 5: 9)

Needless to say, we all of us suffer injustices in adult life. The list of possible examples is virtually endless. But there are some recurring themes, infidelity in relationships, dishonesty in dealing with finances and property, slander, deformation of character etc., etc. It goes without saying that consciously or unconsciously, injustices, and their associated hurts, lead to dysfunctional behaviours, such as difficulties in relationships, addictive and obsessive activities.

Understandably, there are often associated feelings, such as depression, insecurity, anger and resentment. Sometimes embittered feelings are focused on people who caused us pain and others on God for not having afforded protection.

From a Christian point of view, we can ask, how should we deal with the emotional and practical consequences of injustices which have been suffered in the past? This is an important question at the present time when so many people in English speaking countries are coming to terms with the disturbing issue of child sex abuse, especially by members of the clergy and religious orders, and with the related issue of the oppressive and arbitrary exercise of Church authority in the past. I would like to suggest that there is a story in Acts 16: 16-40 which can act as an instructive example of how to deal with such experiences in a positive and liberating way.

Paul and Silas Victims of Painful Injustice

Phillipi was a city in present day northern Greece. It was named after its founder, Philip II of Macedonia. It was under Roman Rule when Paul and Silas visited it in 50-51 A.D. during the apostle to the gentiles' second missionary journey. It was a superstitious place. We are told about a girl with powers of a clairvoyant nature. Apparently she worked for two men who exploited her gift of foretelling the future for financial gain. On a number of occasions she annoyed Paul by interrupting his preaching. Not only did he discern that she was influenced by the spirit of the occult, he delivered her from its malign influence. When her ability to tell fortunes was no longer operative, her two handlers were so angered by their sudden loss of ill-gotten gains that they 'seized Paul and Silas and dragged them into the marketplace to face the authorities .... and said, 'These men are Jews, and are throwing our city into an uproar by advocating customs unlawful for us Romans to accept or practice" Acts 16: 19-21. It is interesting to see that rather than mention the real cause of their indignation, the men slyly exploited Roman dislike of Jewish mores. We are told what happened next: 'The crowd joined in the attack against Paul and Silas, and the magistrates ordered them to be stripped and beaten' Acts 16: 22.

When Paul and Silas received a severe flogging, 'they were thrown into prison, and the jailer was commanded to guard them carefully. Upon receiving such orders, he put them in the inner cell and fastened their feet in the stocks' Acts 16: 23-24. These actions amounted to a gross and painful miscarriage of justice for three reasons. Firstly, Paul and Silas hadn't acted in an illegal way. In fact they had done the woman a favour by freeing her from an oppressive spirit and the unscrupulous exploitation of the two men. Secondly, the accusers intentionally brought spurious, racist charges against the two evangelists. Thirdly, although Paul and Silas, were tried as Jews, they were also Roman citizens. As such, the law clearly stated that they couldn't be sentenced to receive a flogging. But knowledge of their citizenship was deliberately suppressed.

How Paul and Silas Reacted

Paul and Silas were classic victims. Their rights and dignity had been ignored. Instead, they had been falsely accused, physically abused in a humiliating manner, and deprived of their liberty. As they stood there in darkness and in chains, they could feel pain in all their suppurating wounds. How did they react? Did they angrily curse the two men and the local magistrates for treating them in such an unjust and harsh a manner? Did they complain to the Lord for not having protected them? Not a bit of it. Instead of magnifying their problems by focusing on them, we are told that they magnified God by focusing on the glory of the Lord. They offered the Almighty prayers and songs of praise and thanksgiving.

This raises the question, why did they react in such an unusual way? It is highly likely that Paul and Silas were acting in accordance with their faith awareness. Its main tenets had often been adverted to by Paul, and indeed other New Testament authors, in their writings.

Firstly, he was well aware that Jesus had also been the victim of injustice and cruel treatment (cf. 1 Peter 2: 20-23). Pilate, the Roman Governor had said at his trial, 'nothing deserving death has been done by him; *I will therefore* (my italics) chastise him' Luke 23: 15-16. No doubt the two disciples remembered this grossly unfair adjudication. As Paul said in Collossians 1: 24, 'Now I rejoice in my sufferings …and in my flesh I am filling up what is lacking in the afflictions of Christ.'

145

While Paul saw injustice and suffering as evils in themselves, he thought that they could have a silver lining. For instance in Romans 5: 3-5 he stated: 'we also rejoice in our sufferings, because we know that suffering produces perseverance; perseverance, character; and character, hope. And hope does not disappoint us, because God has poured out his love into our hearts by the Holy Spirit, whom he has given us.' Again in 2 Corinthians 1: 4 Paul testified that God: 'comforts us in all our troubles, so that we can comfort those in any trouble with the comfort we ourselves have received from God.'

Secondly, Paul was aware that the injustice and pain which he and Silas were enduring in union with Christ, though evil in themselves, were embraced by the merciful providence of God. As he said of believers like himself and his companion: 'we know that in all things (i.e. good and bad alike) God works for the good of those who love him, who have been called according to his purpose' Romans 8: 28. In another place, Paul made the profound observation: 'the gift is not like the transgression. For if by Adam's transgression the many died, how much more did the grace of God and the gracious gift of the one person Jesus Christ overflow for the many' Romans 5: 15. So Paul and Silas believed that, where the sin of their unjust oppressors abounded, the grace of God would more abound, not only for them as victims, but also for their victimisers.

Thirdly, in the light of the first two points, Paul believed that Christians should praise and thank God in all circumstances, good and bad alike, in the belief that they are the springboards to future blessing. As Chapter 6 points out, he had this conviction in mind when he said: 'pray continually; give thanks in all circumstances, for this is God's will for you in Christ Jesus,' 1 Thessallonians 5: 17-18. In Ephesians 5: 20 he added: 'always give thanks to God the Father for everything, in the name of our Lord Jesus Christ.' In Phillippians 4: 6 he said: 'Do not be anxious about anything, but in everything, by prayer and petition, with thanksgiving, present your requests to God.' Finally, in Collossians 3: 17 we read: 'And whatever you do, whether in word or deed, do it all in the name of the Lord Jesus, giving thanks to God the Father through him.' In the light of these interrelated points, it is not too surprising that Paul and Silas were praying and singing hymns in accordance with the teaching of Collossians 3: 16: 'sing psalms, hymns and spiritual songs .'

The Liberating Power of Praise and Thanksgiving

Luke tells us that when the two disciples were worshipping God: 'the other prisoners were listening to them' Acts 16: 25. Presumably their reaction was one of puzzled amazement and awed curiosity. It had a liberating effect. It says in Psalm 22: 3 that the Lord lives in the praises of the people. Whenever we lift the, metaphorical, chalice of our adoration, God fills it with the Spirit's liberating presence. There were intimations of this dynamic in a number of Old Testament stories. For instance, when the three young men praised God in the fiery furnace, instead of being burnt they were set free (cf. Daniel 3: 24). When Jonah praised God in the belly of the whale, instead of being lost at sea he was coughed up on the shore (cf. Jonah 2:9-10). In Acts 16: 26 it was much the same. As they were, un-selfconsciously, praising God: 'Suddenly there was such a violent earthquake that the foundations of the prison were shaken. At once all the prison doors flew open, and everybody's chains came loose.' Not only were the disciples liberated from the oppressive consequences of human malice and injustice by the liberating power and providence of God, so were those who were participating vicariously by merely listening to their prayers of praise and thanksgiving.

Victimisers are Liberated Also

When the jailer, who had participated in the injustice and oppression inflicted on Paul and Silas, thought that his prisoners had escaped, he was immediately tempted to commit suicide. This reaction tells us something about the abuser. He was a vulnerable man. He lived to do his duty. As soon as he failed to do so, he lost his will to live. This was quite an anomaly. Although, Paul and Silas were chained in the inner darkness of the prison they were free in Spirit, whereas, the jailer who was ostensibly free, was really enchained in the darkness of his inner emptiness and despair. Luke seems to be saying, in a metaphorical way, that the injustices perpetrated by abusers are often the expression of their own inner pathologies and pain.

When Paul saw that the jailer was about to take his own life, he shouted: 'Don't harm yourself! We are all here!' Acts 16: 28. This reaction indicates that Paul bore no ill-will or resentment against his abuser. Then we are informed that: 'The jailer called for lights, rushed in and fell trembling before Paul and Silas. He then brought them out and asked, 'Sirs, what must I do to be saved?' With this vital question, the abuser is admitting that there is a great deficit in his life. Paradoxically, the abusing jailer asks the abused prisoners how to escape from the chains of his own inner oppression. 'They replied, 'Believe in the Lord Jesus, and you will be saved - you and your household' Acts 16: 28-31. Just as the crucified Jesus had gone 'and preached to the spirits in prison' 1 Pet 3: 19, so Paul and Silas evangelised the Roman jailer, and subsequently his family. The topsy-turvy nature of the story continues when we are told that the person who formerly inflicted unjust abuse, became their healer. 'At that hour of the night the jailer took them and washed their wounds' Acts 16: 33.

Assertion of Personal Dignity and Rights

Although Paul and Silas didn't get angry about the wrongs inflicted upon them, it wasn't because they were whimpish or lacking in self-assertiveness due to low self-esteem. We know this because the next morning the jailer informed the two disciples that the local magistrates had said that they were free to leave. But Paul said .... 'They beat us publicly without a trial, even though we are Roman citizens, and threw us into prison. And now do they want to get rid of us quietly? No! Let them come themselves and escort us out' Acts 16: 37. Clearly, as a man who had experienced the liberating and divinising effects of the free gift of the Holy Spirit given to him in his neediness, Paul was asserting his dignity and rights, as a Roman citizen yes, but as a citizen of the Kingdom of God also. Whenever, a person experiences inner liberation and healing as a result of the action of divine grace his or her sense of worth is also restored.

From Prison to Praise

This New Testament story is instructive in so far as it proposes a template, a reliable Christian method of dealing with the injustices and hurts that are an inevitable part of life. In modern times there have been a number of well known examples of Christians following this scriptural example with liberating effects. For instance, when Protestant pastor, Richard Wurmbrant, was unjustly imprisoned for 14 years by the Rumanian communists, he read the beatitude which promises: 'Blessed are you when people insult you, persecute you and falsely say all kinds of evil against you because of me. Rejoice and be glad, because great is your reward in heaven, for in the same way they persecuted the prophets who were before you' Matthew 5: 11-12. Although he didn't feel like doing so, Wurmbrant decided to act in faith on the basis of these inspired words.

In his book *Tortured for Christ* pastor Wurmbrant said: 'I hear so many saying of my years in prison, 'This poor Wurmbrant. He has suffered so much.' There was suffering, but in truth there was also such joy to be with Christ. We sang in prison because Christ was alive in us. Many Christians sing once a week. We sang in prison every day. We sang accompanied by musical instruments. The Communists in our Romanian prison..... gave every Christian a musical instrument. They did not give us violins or mandolins..... Instead they put chains on our hands and feet. We discovered that chains are splendid musical instruments. Not only did we sing, but we also danced in prison. The guards looked through a peephole so they could see what was happening. When they saw me dancing they were sure that I had gone mad. They were ordered to treat madmen very well because madmen would bang on the door and shout, destroying the order in prison. Immediately the guard opened the door, entered, patted me on the shirt and said, 'I'll bring you something good, only behave yourself, sit quietly and I will bring it to you.' He brought back a loaf of bread and a piece of cheese ...Jesus says that when you are oppressed, rejoice and leap for joy! I leaped for joy and He brought me all these things, a big loaf of bread and even cheese and sugar ...When anything troubles you, sing a song.' Ezra the priest was so right when he said to his grieving people: 'do not be grieved, for the joy of the Lord is your strength' Nehemiah 8: 10.

I believe that Christian individuals and groups, who are aware of being the victims of injustices and associated hurts in the past, can also experience liberation and healing by imitating the example of Paul and Silas.

1. Go down the steps from rational awareness into the

subterranean recesses of memory where you feel bound in the darkness by the hurts and injustices you have experienced.

2. While you may acknowledge to God that you feel a sense of loss, hurt, shame, guilt, anger and bitter resentment, act on the basis of your faith convictions rather than your negative feelings.

3. Having accepted that divine providence has allowed you to participate in the injustices and hurts inflicted on Christ, praise and thank God in the firm belief that these evils will not have the last word. It will be spoken by God, and it will be a therapeutic word of liberation.

4. Believe that as you experience inner healing and peace, God's grace will so abound as to mysteriously bless those, living or dead, who have wronged you. It may even be that they will contribute, in one way or another, to your healing and growth.

5. As a result of this kind of approach expect that your sense of inner dignity and healthy assertiveness will be restored.

6. Do not be surprised that when you acknowledge God's benevolent sovereignty by means of praise and thanksgiving, not only may your oppressors be blessed, they, in turn, may be used by God to bring you blessings also.

Conclusion

We are living in a culture where many people are coming to terms with the injustices and hurts they have experienced in the past. This awareness of inner pain can make them either bitter or better. The outcome will largely depend on the way in which they handle those issues. If they do so in the Christian manner described in Acts 16: 16-40, I am convinced that it will lead to healing, liberation and inner peace.

Chapter 21

The New Age Movement Evaluated

The name, 'New Age,' has an astrological origin. According to its devotees we are about to leave the age of Pisces. i.e. the Christian era, which for the last 2000 years has been characterised by a lot of violence. They maintain that we are about to enter the Age of Aquarius, i.e. the era of universal religion, which will be a time of peace, harmony, and wholeness. The New Age movement, with its distinctive beliefs and practices, has become increasingly influential over the last thirty years. It is hard to describe because it has no fixed creed or identifiable organisation. Someone has, rightly, observed that understanding it is like trying to wrestle with a jelly. As soon as you think you have got it under control, the shape of the whole thing changes and you have to start again.

The New Age Movement Evaluated

A Pastoral Problem

As a priest I have noted different ways in which the New Age movement has been impinging upon the Catholic Church. For example, when I look at lists of forthcoming events in some retreat centres, it becomes apparent that a number of them, such as Ti Chi, the Enneagram and Dream Therapy, are not of the traditional Christian kind. Many people contact me, by phone and in person, to ask whether I think modern practices such as aromatherapy, Reiki healing, reflexology, the Sila Method of mind control, and Yoga are compatible with Christian belief. I have also noticed how some conservative and fundamentalist Christian writers are highly critical of anything to do with the New Age, seeing it as either pagan or diabolical in nature.

Many bishops and pastors have, understandably, been perplexed by all these developments. As a result, a number of them turned to Rome for help. They wanted answers to a series of questions. What exactly is the New Age movement? What are its distinctive beliefs and practices? To what extent is it compatible with official Christian teaching? Can the Church learn anything helpful from the New Age movement?

Vatican Guidelines

Recently a discussion document entitled, *Jesus Christ the Bearer of the Water of Life: A Christian Reflection on the New Age* was published by the Vatican. The authors say that it is an interim response, a sort of green paper. It has two aims. Firstly, 'it is an invitation to understand the New Age and to engage in a genuine dialogue with those who are influenced by New Age thought.' Secondly, it is 'meant as a guide for Catholics in preaching the Gospel and teaching the faith at any level within the Church.' Apparently, when members of the Church have had an opportunity to offer feed-back on what it says, a final, more definitive version will be published.

Before I studied the document I wondered whether it would be written in a narrow-minded or an open-minded, Catholic way. I was reassured when I read: 'It is essential to try to understand the New Age correctly, in order to evaluate it fairly, and avoid creating a caricature. It would be unwise and untrue to say that everything connected with the New Age movement is good, or that everything about it is bad.' The document offers a well-informed, balanced and sympathetic description of the world-view informing the New Age movement. For example, speaking of its beliefs, it says succinctly:

1.   'The world, including the human race, constitutes an expression of a higher, more comprehensive divine nature.

2.   Hidden within each human being is a higher divine self, which is a manifestation of the higher, more comprehensive divine nature.

3.   This higher nature can be awakened and can become the centre of the individual's everyday life.

4.   This awakening is the reason for the existence of

each individual life.'

The document concludes with a helpful glossary of 32 New Age terms, such as channelling, crystals, karma, Feng-shui and reincarnation, while briefly describing what each of them means.

What are the main conclusions of the Pontifical document? Firstly, it sees the New Age movement as a laudable reaction to the materialism and rationalism of a good deal of western culture. Secondly, it is well attuned to the subjectivism of postmodern culture. Thirdly, it is attracting many people who are keen to have a meaningful spiritual life but who are disillusioned, for one reason or another, with the institutional churches. Fourthly, rather than being a new phenomenon, it sees the New Age as a reappearance of ancient Gnosticism which talked, nearly 2000 years ago, about achieving salvation through higher states of consciousness. Whereas early Gnosticism synthesised Christian, Platonic and pagan beliefs, the New Age version adds in contemporary elements such as science, psychology and spiritualism. But just as many Gnostic beliefs were not acceptable in early Christianity, so many New Age beliefs are unacceptable in modern Christianity.

Critique of New Age Beliefs

The document notes many of the reasons why. Firstly, God is not an impersonal energy as New Age thinking suggests. Secondly, when the New Age says that Jesus Christ is not God, but one of the many historical manifestations of the cosmic and universal Christ, it is quite mistaken. Thirdly, whereas the New Age movement believes that we save ourselves by raising our levels of consciousness by using man made techniques, Christians believe, that we are justified by grace through faith in Christ and not by our own unaided efforts. Fourthly, Christians reject the New Age notion of sin as merely an imperfect form of knowledge which can be redressed by means of New Age methods.

Thankfully, this very helpful document from Rome has identified the theological and ethical implications of the New Age movement and challenged its rejection of important Christian doctrines. However, it says that Christians need to avoid a prejudiced rejection of every idea and practice associated with New Age spirituality. As *Jesus Christ the Bearer of the Water of Life* says: 'the relationship of the person, group, practice or commodity to the central tenets of Christianity is what counts.' If you are interested in the New Age movement from a Catholic point of view, you would be well advised to read this informative document which can be downloaded from the Vatican website.

Conclusion

In a recent book entitled *The Broken Image*, I suggested in a chapter entitled, 'Popular Devotion and Primal Piety' that, just as New Age Spirituality is a non-Christian response to secular postmodernism, so Pentecostal/Charismatic spirituality is an interesting Christian response to the same phenomenon.

However, Charismatics have to be on their guard, so that they do not assume the world view that informs much of New Age Spirituality. Rather, they need to discover parallel beliefs within the Christian tradition. For example, whereas New Age Spirituality believes that each person can use psycho-technologies, such as depth psychology, to become consciously aware of their divine nature, Christians maintain in the words of par. 3.5 of *Jesus Christ Bearer of the Water of Life* that: 'the Christian understanding of divinisation, comes about not through our own efforts alone, but with the assistance of God's grace working in and through us. It inevitably involves an initial awareness of incompleteness and even sinfulness, in no way an exaltation of the self. Furthermore, it unfolds as an introduction into the life of the Trinity, a perfect case of distinction at the heart of unity; *it is synergy rather than fusion* (my italics).'

Chapter 22

Reading Scripture and Religious Experience

Some time ago, I did a year-long course in spiritual direction. As would-be directors we were told that rather than concentrating on talk or thought about God we would be better off focusing on people's religious experience, that is, their conscious awareness of the One who chooses to reveal the Divine presence and purposes to us. When I came home I thought a lot about the importance and nature of religious experience.

We can begin by noting the fact that in our postmodern culture, where many people have lost confidence in objective truth, experience is what people trust. A few years ago I formulated the following statement which tries to encapsulate a paradigm shift that has taken place in our culture. In the postmodern world, the centre of gravity in Christianity is shifting from the experience of religious authority to the authority of religious experience. As the Pope remarked in one of his encyclicals, 'people of today trust more in experience than they do in dogma.'

The Nature of Religious Experience

When I reflected on the nature of religious experience I could see that it consisted of four interrelated aspects.

Firstly, it begins in desire. Down the centuries, great spiritual writers have agreed that grace prompted desires for ultimate meaning and God are of great importance in the Christian life. They have pointed to Gospel texts which make it clear that Jesus focused on such desires in his ministry. For example, in John 1: 35-38 John the Baptist tells two young men that Jesus is the Lamb of God. 'When the two disciples heard him say this, they followed Jesus. Turning around, Jesus saw them following and asked, 'What do you want?' Jesus asked this all-important question because he realised that God reveals his purposes in and through such desires. Thus St Augustine could write: 'The things you desire you cannot see yet. But the desire gives you the capacity, so that when it does happen that you see, you may be fulfilled... this is our life, to be motivated by holy desire. But we are motivated by holy desire only in so far as we have cut off our longings from the love of the world. I have already pointed out how it is necessary to empty that which is to be filled. You are to be filled with good, pour out the bad.'

Secondly, desire for God is expressed in self-forgetful attention. Needless to say, attention to scripture is the best way of opening oneself to the presence and purposes of God. As Proverbs 4: 22-23 tells us: 'My child, be attentive to my words; incline your ear to my sayings. Do not let them escape from your sight; keep them within your heart. For they are life to those who find them, and healing to all their flesh.' One of the best ways of paying attention to God's self revelation in scripture is by engaging in *Lectio Divina*, i.e. sacred reading, a prayer method that can be traced back to St Benedict.

Thirdly, desire filled attention can lead to contemplative moments of revelation. In scripture we have a promise that those who seek God will find God. As Jeremiah 33: 3 says: 'Call to me and I will answer you, and will tell you great and hidden things that you have not known.' Again in Isaiah 48: 6-8 we read: 'From now on I will tell you of new things, of hidden things unknown to you. They are created now, and not long ago; you have not heard of them before today. So you cannot say, 'Yes, I knew of them.' You have neither heard nor understood; from of old your ear has not been open.' When this happens God's alive and active word leaps off the page into the heart with subjective relevance, meaning and power. As a result the person has a new awareness of the presence and will of the Lord, one that evokes faith in the heart (Cf.

Romans 10: 17).

Lastly, the revelation of the God's loving presence and intentions leads to three interrelated effects.

• Firstly, the person will experience feelings of consolation such as peace and joy which are stirred up by the Spirit's activity in and through God's anointed word.
• Secondly, the person can respond in a prayerful way e.g. by thanking and praising God.
• Thirdly, the person can respond in a more practical manner e.g. by being for others what God is for him or her.

A Scriptural Example

An interesting passage in Acts 8: 26-40 illustrates the inter-connection of these four points. It describes both the geographical and spiritual journey of an Ethiopian eunuch who was an official in the court of queen Candece. Incidentally, the word Ethiopia may have originally meant black. According to eminent scripture scholar, Raymond Brown, in his *Introduction to the New Testament*, it is possible that this negro was from Egypt or the upper Sudan.

1. Desire
Wherever he was from, the court official certainly had the kind of transcendental desire that can lead to religious experience. Why else would he have gone so far to worship in Jerusalem. We are also told that when he was returning from Jerusalem he was travelling

along the desert road, one that did not seem to be in use anymore. The fact that it was deserted, lonely, and arid seemed to be a metaphorical image of the official's inner state. In spite of his wealth, education and influential position at court, deep down he was aware that there was something missing in his life, perhaps a joyful sense of ultimate belonging. We are not told whether he was a Jew or a God-fearer, i.e. a gentile who accepted the main teachings of Judaism. One way or the other, the Lord had promised that anyone who was motivated by desires like those experienced by the court official, would never be in vain: 'you will call upon me and come and pray to me, and I will listen to you. You will seek me and find me when you seek me with all your heart' Jeremiah 29: 12-14.

2. Attention

Apparently as he travelled along in his carriage, instead of watching where he was going, he let the reins go limp and trusted that the horse would find its own way while he attentively read Isaiah 53: 7-8 from a scroll he had. As he did so, Philip, the evangelist, was led by an angel to go down that same road and to make contact. In Greek the word angel literally means messenger of the Lord. As Hebrews 13: 2 advised: 'Do not forget to entertain strangers, for by so doing some people have entertained angels without knowing it.' It may be that some member of the Christian community had given Philip a prophetic word of guidance. He in turn became the eunuch's, God appointed, angel.

Philip was an obedient man. From a human point of view there wasn't much chance of meeting anyone on such a deserted road. But as providence had fore-ordained, the unexpected happened, when he saw the approaching carriage. We are told that he ran up to it and heard the man reading. He asked if he understood the passage. 'How can I,' he said, 'unless someone explains it to me?' Then the eunuch listened attentively to what Philip had to say. The evangelist proceeded, on the Church's behalf, to tell him that it was a prophetic anticipation of the future coming of the Suffering Servant. Then he shared the good news about Jesus, the Son of God, who had died and risen in order that sins might be forgiven. He would also have told him how the risen Lord pours out the Holy Spirit on those who are baptised, thereby enabling them to grasp how wide and long and high and deep is the unrestricted and unconditional love of God, that surpasses human understanding, so that he might be filled with the presence of God.

3. Revelation

I suspect that the eunuch was deeply moved when Philip told him about Jesus; how he had suffered great injustice at the hands of the Jewish and Roman authorities, had been humiliated in public, and died without heirs. He could identify with the Lord. He had suffered the childhood injustice of involuntary castration. As a result of his appearance and high pitched voice he had often endured ridicule, and because of his violently enforced infertility he could have no children. He could see that Jesus, as God's son, had completely identified with his suffering and shame as an outsider. Like him, Jesus had suffered violent injustice and had died in his prime without children. This was his moment of revelation, of spiritual awakening. Inwardly, he felt accepted and loved by Jesus.

4. Response

His response was instantaneous and wholehearted. Not only did he believe in the Good News, he immediately asked to be baptised. 'Then both Philip and the eunuch went down into the water and Philip baptised him.' At last, his search was over. Finally, he felt the joy of ultimate belonging. Then as mysteriously as he had appeared, Philip disappeared. We are told that the eunuch continued on his way, rejoicing. One would suspect that when he got home he not only witnessed to his new found faith by his happiness but also imitated Philip by telling others about the way in which the good news had transformed his life.

Conclusion

Philip had been an effective and archetypal evangelist because, from first to last, he had been led by the Spirit. Instead of preaching or imposing his agenda, he had listened sensitively to the eunuch and responded to his questions. As a model evangelist, he was able, in this way, to satisfy the man's God prompted desire to know God.

When one reads the account of Jesus, the Stranger,

meeting the two disciples on the road to Emmaus, it quickly becomes evident that it has a good deal in common with the passage about the Ethiopian eunuch. In both the scriptures are recalled and then explained in an inspired way by the God sent stranger. Both explanations lead to revelation and faith and are followed by the disappearance of the strangers in a mysterious way. We know that when the two disciples came to faith in the risen Lord, they returned to Jerusalem to share the good news with the grieving disciples, and as suggested already, we can presume that when the eunuch came to faith in the risen Lord, he returned home and shared the good news with his fellow courtiers.

Chapter 23

The Gift of Generosity

Recently, circumstances led me to think about generosity for three reasons. Firstly, I had accepted a position in Aid to the Church in Need, a charitable organisation which gives financial assistance to Catholic and Orthodox groups in poorer parts of the world. All the money it distributes comes from the contributions of generous people. Secondly, around this time I had been particularly moved and edified by the repeated generosity of one particular donor, a woman who runs a successful business. She gave surprisingly large donations on a regular basis. Thirdly, around this time I heard that a relative had left me a modest amount of money and I wondered what I would do with it. When I was thinking about these related points, I felt I had been illumined by the Holy

Spirit. It occurred to me with great clarity and conviction that the charism of being generous to others, as God is generous to us, lies at the heart of Christian and therefore Charismatic spirituality.

Divine Bounty

I suspect that, as many of us get older, we become ever more consciously aware of the fact that every aspect of life is pure gift. The existence of the universe in all its macrocosmic grandeur and microcosmic detail, is the Gift of God. This is equally true of our own lives, endowed, as they are, with natural talents and unmerited graces. Clearly, these blessings are reflections of the prodigious generosity of the Holy Trinity. Not content with sharing fellowship with one another, the generosity of the Father, Son and Holy Spirit spills over in the creation of the endless wonders of the angelic and natural orders in which we participate.

There is a good example of this in Mark 6: 34. Jesus and the apostles had been working hard. The crowds needing ministry were so great they hadn't had an opportunity to eat. When they tried to take time off by themselves, large numbers of people anticipated where they were going, and were waiting for them when they arrived. As soon as Jesus saw them, sad and dejected, like sheep without a shepherd, he didn't get frustrated or ignore their needs. Instead, he felt compassion for them and generously began to teach and to heal them. As his death on the cross demonstrated, in a definitive way, Jesus was even willing to sacrifice his life so that sinners might be saved.

Jesus on Divine Beneficence

Jesus had a profound sense of the generosity of God as the expression of God's glory, greatness and goodness. He spoke about it on a number of occasions. It was this awareness that informed all his teaching about the efficacy of prayers of petition and supplication. In Luke 15: 31 the Prodigal Father said to his elder son: 'You are with me always, all I have is yours.' In other words, 'if you related to me your loving father in a trusting rather than a dutiful way, you would realise that I'm unstinting in my generosity, there is no good gift I would withhold from you. You could have claimed the ring of my authority, worn the cloak of honour, the shoes of freedom, and killed the fatted calf whenever you liked.' On another occasion Jesus drew attention to the way God's generosity found expression in extravagant giving when he said: 'If you parents, who are evil, know how to give good gifts to your children, how much more will your Father who is in heaven give good things to those who ask him' Matthew 7: 11. In other words, if imperfect parents often go to great lengths to help their children, how much more will the perfect Father in heaven be willing to generously do what is best for his children.

Later in the New Testament St Paul also talked about the generosity of God. In Romans 8: 32 he observed: 'If God has given us his Son would he not give us all things in him.' In other words, if the Father in his unimaginable goodness has given us Jesus as his greatest gift, why should he withhold any lesser gifts? As St Paul said repeatedly: 'my God will supply every need of yours according to his riches in glory in Christ Jesus ......Blessed be the God and Father of our Lord Jesus Christ, who has blessed us in Christ with every spiritual blessing in the heavenly places ....the same Lord is Lord of all and is generous to all who call on him' Phillippians 4: 19; Ephesians 1: 3; Romans 10: 12.

Gratitude

When people become aware of the generosity of God, two responses are called for; prayerful thanks and practical generosity. Firstly, we thank God for all the natural and supernatural gifts that have been lavished upon us. As the messenger Raphael said to Tobit and his son Tobias: 'Praise God and give thanks to him; exalt him and give thanks to him in the presence of the living for the good things He has done for you. Bless and extol His name, worthily declaring the works of God. Do not be slow to give him thanks' Tobit 12: 6. As we saw in Chapters 6 and 20, St Paul not only thanked God repeatedly, he urged people of faith to: 'pray continually; give thanks in all circumstances, for this is God's will for you in Christ Jesus,' 1 Thessalonians 5: 17-18. Needless to say the Eucharist, the greatest sign and source of God's abundant generosity, is also the supreme act of Christian thanksgiving.

Practical Generosity

Whenever a Christian becomes experientially aware of

an attribute of God, implicit in that awareness is the spiritual imperative, 'be for others what God is for you.' For instance, 'if you have found God to be generous, be generous yourself.' Jesus had enunciated this, all important principle, in Luke 6: 38. Having encouraged the disciples to imitate the generosity of the Father, he said: 'Give, and it will be given to you. A good measure, pressed down, shaken together, running over, will be put into your lap; for the measure you give will be the measure you get back.' In a word, we need to be unstinting in our responses to the gift of God's grace by being generous to people.

For instance, we can be more generous in our loving, both in terms of interpersonal relationships and practical service. Generosity in relationships, involves such things as being willing to give time to people; listening to them with empathy, and sharing openly and honestly with them when it seems appropriate. Whenever hurts are experienced, as inevitably they will, the offended parties need to be generous in offering forgiveness. Generosity in the form of practical service, is ideally, an expression of a loving relationship rather than a dutiful substitute for it. It is a matter of putting the Golden Rule of Matthew 7: 12 into action, by escaping the gravitational pull of self-absorption to sensitively give people what they need, for example; encouragement, practical help, or financial assistance.

Generosity to the Poor and Needy

The author of 1 Timothy 6: 10 warned that 'the love of

money is the root of all kinds of evil.' Not surprisingly, the scriptures say that the main antidote to greed is financial generosity. Jesus made it clear in the story of the widow's mite that it wasn't the size of a financial contribution that was important, but rather the degree of personal sacrifice involved. The evangelist tells us that, having observed the widow put two coins into the treasury, 'he called his disciples and said to them, 'Truly I tell you, this poor widow has put in more than all those who are contributing to the treasury. For all of them have contributed out of their abundance; but she out of her poverty has put in everything she had, all she had to live on'' Mark 12: 43-44.

The scriptures make it clear that generosity to the less well off is particularly praiseworthy . As Deuteronomy 15: 10-11 says: 'Give liberally and be ungrudging when you do so, for on this account the Lord your God will bless you in all your work and in all that you undertake. Since there will never cease to be some in need on the earth, I therefore command you, 'Open your hand to the poor and needy neighbour in your land.' In other words, if you want to continue to experience God's bountiful gifts and graces, you must be prepared to: 'Give as you have made up your mind, not reluctantly or under compulsion, for God loves a cheerful giver. And God is able to provide you with every blessing in abundance, so that by always having enough of everything, you may share abundantly in every good work' 2 Corinthians 9: 7-8. The author of 1 Timothy 6: 17-18 echoed this sentiment when he said: 'As for those who in the present age are rich, command them not to be haughty, or to set their hopes on the uncertainty of riches, but rather on God who richly provides us with everything for our enjoyment. They are to do good, to be rich in good works, generous, and ready to share.' Proverbs 22: 9 rightly declares that: 'Those who are generous are blessed, for they share their bread with the poor." In the gospels, Jesus makes it clear why this is so: 'Truly I tell you, just as you did not do it to one of the least of these, you did not do it to me.' Matthew 25: 45

It is evident that Paul encouraged the better off members of the gentile Church to be generous to those who were needy, especially those in Jerusalem. He said: 'Contribute to the needs of the saints' Romans 12: 13.   A little later he mentioned why the gentile converts should be generous to their Jewish co-religionists: 'They owe it to them; for if the Gentiles have come to share in their spiritual blessings, they ought also to be of service to them in material things' Romans 15: 27. However, he counselled moderation in giving: 'I do not mean that there should be relief for others and pressure on you, but it is a question of a fair balance between your present abundance and their need, so that their abundance may be for your need, in order that there may be a fair balance. As it is written, 'The one who had much did not have too much, and the one who had little did not have too little' 2 Corinthians 8: 13-15.   Some time later Paul went on to link the related notions of Christian generosity and thanksgiving when he said: 'You will be enriched in every way for your great generosity, which will produce thanksgiving to God through us; for the rendering of this ministry not only supplies the needs of the saints but also overflows with many thanksgivings to God' 2 Corinthians 9: 11-12. Needless to say, these principles are relevant at the local and universal level in the contemporary Church, where there are many situations of need.

Conclusion

From a human point of view generosity is not only a participation in God's providential provision, it is a sign of nobility of character. The word 'generous' in English is derived from the Latin *generosus*, which refers to the benevolence and kindness characteristic of those of aristocratic birth. From a Christian point of view generosity is a fruit of the Spirit (cf. Gal 5: 22). If Christians want to grow in grace they need, not only to experience the generosity of God, but also to respond quickly, generously, and appropriately, either in a spiritual way e.g. by devoting more time to personal prayer, or in a practical way e.g. by engaging in voluntary work.

Traditional Irish spirituality encouraged this kind of practical giving. For example, there is a Gaelic folk tale which describes how, in the Autumn, a farmer stored seed potatoes in a large bin with a view to using them for the sowing in the Spring. He warned his wife not to use any of them. But when poor people came to the door during the cold Winter months, she felt sorry for them and gave each one a few potatoes from the bin. In the Spring, when the time for sowing arrived, the woman was on tenterhooks because she knew that the bin was nearly empty. But when her husband opened it, surprise, surprise, it was full to the brim with first class seed potatoes! The message is obvious, in giving we receive, even to the point of miracles. Quoting words of Jesus, that are not recorded in the gospels, St Paul testified: 'It is more blessed to give than to receive' Acts 20: 35.

Chapter 24

An Examen of Consciousness

Speaking about contemporary culture, Pope Paul VI once made the pertinent observation that:

'Today our psychology is turned outward too much. The external scene is so absorbing that our attention is mainly directed outside; we are nearly always absent from our personal abode. We are unable to meditate or pray. We cannot silence the hubbub inside, due to outside interests, images and passions. There is no quiet, holy space in the heart for the flame of Pentecost.'

Like the prodigal son, who came to his senses, an examen of consciousness, enables a person to return home to the inner chamber of the heart, and God's activity within it, by means of a reflection exercise.
(a) Rather than being an examination of conscience i.e. an itemised assessment of wrongdoing from a

Christian point of view, an examen of consciousness aims to focus attention on God-given desires, and how one did or did not respond to them. It seeks to notice what may be inhibiting them.

(b) It enables a person to become aware of the presence and inspirations of the Lord. It also looks at a person's reactions and responses to such revelations.

(c) In the words of I John 4: I, it develops the ability to 'test the spirits to see whether they are of God.' St. Ignatius of Loyola wrote in par. 32 of his *Spiritual Exercises*:

'There are three kinds of thought in the mind, namely: one which is strictly my own, and arises wholly from my own free will; two others which come from without, the one from the good Spirit, the other from the Evil One.'

It is worth noting that St Ignatius of Loyola, considered the regular examen of consciousness was so important in the life of any apostolic person that s/he should not omit it except for a serious reason, such as serving God's greater glory.

A Discernment Exercise

• Relax your body.
• Calm your mind and imagination.
• Affirm in faith that God is present.
• Consider these words of Cardinal Newman:

'God's presence is not discerned at the time it is upon us, but afterwards when we look back upon what is gone and over.'

• Ask the Holy Spirit to guide your discernment exercise:

'Lord, you enlighten every heart. Enlighten mine to recognise how you have been drawing me to yourself. Help me to appreciate your Presence and to distinguish those inspirations that came from You, and those that came from either myself or from the Evil One.'

Discerning the Presence of the Lord

1. During the recent past, when were you most aware of the Lord's presence? Was it at Mass, when praying, reading the scriptures, enjoying nature, talking with a friend, etc? Briefly describe the incident.

2. What did you experience when the Lord revealed Himself to you? Was it joy, awe, peace, fear, hope, encouragement, etc? Did you tell the Lord what you felt?

3. What did you notice about the Person of the Lord when he revealed Himself to you that would account for the feelings evoked within you? Was He compassionate, accepting, attentive, understanding, loving, angry, etc? Try and describe the God of your experience in a few words.

4. How did you decide to respond to the revelation of the Lord?

(a) Did it find expression in a prayerful way, e.g. in gratitude and praise?

(b) Did it find expression in any kind of resolution, e.g. to be reconciled to someone, to avoid temptation, to work for justice etc?

Discerning Positive from Negative Inspirations

(A) Were you aware of any promptings or inspirations from the Holy Spirit in the recent past? Did you respond to them or not? (See St. Vincent's comments below)

(B) Did you experience any kind of negative inspiration, feeling, attitude, mood, desire which may have led to a sinful thought, word or deed in the recent past? If so, tell the Lord that you are sorry for having saddened the Holy Spirit, and ask for His forgiveness with confidence.

Thank God for the graces He has given you in the recent past and ask His blessing upon your future.

Concluding Observations

• *How Often Should The Discernment Method Be Used?*

As often as you like. But most people find that once a week enough. Anything more could be impractical.

• *How Much Time Should Be Spent on The Exercise?*

Normally, between five and fifteen minutes will be sufficient. During a retreat one might spend a bit longer.

• *Should The Results of The Discernment Be Written Down?*

Strictly speaking, it isn't necessary to write down the results of the discernment exercise. However, to do so can have distinct advantages.

(1) To express something on paper has the effect of impressing it upon the mind and memory.

(2) To review one's notes after a few months could reveal interesting and important trends, that might otherwise be overlooked.

(3) If one is fortunate to have a spiritual director, notes of the discernment exercise can be very useful as a basis for conversation.

(4) During times of darkness and desolation, the recorded account of past graces and consolations can be a source of encouragement.

(5) The written highlights of the discernment process can be used as the starting points for future periods of prayer.

St Vincent de Paul suggested in a talk on *True Inspirations and Illusions* 17th Oct. 1659, that there are four reliable ways of distinguishing true from false inspirations:

(1) Was the prompting contrary to the commandments of God, Church or the state?

(2) Was it contrary to one's life commitments e.g. married or religious vows?

(3) Was there an element of superstition present?

(4) Was the prompting/inspiration peaceful or troublesome? St Vincent observed: 'The Spirit of God is a spirit of peace, a gentle light which infuses itself into the soul without doing it any violence. It's action is sweet and agreeable and inclines us to seek whatever concerns the greater glory of God.' St Vincent said

that: 'If a person is graciously, peacefully and quietly receptive to the advice given to him or her by a person exercising legitimate authority, and takes account of it, that is a sign that there is no illusion whatever in what s/he does.'

Chapter 25

A Charismatic Check-up

Many of us have an annual check-up. When the results become available, the doctor usually gives us a pep talk and recommends life-changes such as dieting and taking exercise. While it is good to take care of the body, in this way, it is even more important to care for the soul. Surely, we need regular spiritual check-ups. They should look at important aspects of our spiritual lives, with a view to ascertaining what changes might be needed. This questionnaire focuses on three outstanding characteristics of charismatic spirituality, being filled, guided and empowered by the Spirit.

A Questionnaire

Where applicable indicate whether your answer is:

- Never   = 0
- Sometimes = 1
- Often   = 2
- Always   = 3

1.   At some point you experienced a spiritual awakening, one that enabled you to have a new, personal awareness of the length and breadth, the height and depth of the unconditional love of Christ for you. Have you had subsequent in-fillings that have strengthened that sense of God's merciful love?

2.   A spiritual awakening is often associated with the granting of the charismatic gifts mentioned in 1 Corinthians 12: 8-10. If you received one or more of the charisms when you were filled with the Spirit or afterwards, e.g. the gift of praying in tongues, do you exercise them as much now as you once did?

3.   Charismatic spirituality is scripture based. The Holy Spirit leads those who prayerfully reflect upon it into the truth about God and God's purposes. Do you find that when you read the scriptures the word of God, which is true in itself, regularly leaps alive off the page into your heart with such inner meaning and relevance, that it guides your everyday actions?

4.   The exhortation, 'Walk by the Spirit' in Galations 5: 16 is the key to an inspired Christian ethic. The spiritual guidance required to carry out this injunction, can come in different ways, such as an inner prompting, a twinge of conscience, a prophetic word

of knowledge etc. Are you sensitive and docile to such forms of guidance?

5.	The gift of discernment of spirits enables you to identify the origin and orientation of your inspirations. Those that come from God, and lead to God, are prompted by the Holy Spirit and will be associated with feelings of consolation, such as joy and peace. Those that come from ourselves or the Evil Spirit, will sooner or later lead to feelings of desolation, such as sadness and dissatisfaction. Are you reflective enough to notice what spirits are motivating you?

6.	St Ignatius of Loyola pointed out that God may withdraw the consolation of the Spirit as a result of such things as spiritual laziness, neglect of prayer, lack of effort in resisting temptation, or because the person is focusing on the consolations of God rather than the God of consolation. When you suffer from desolation of spirit, do you prayerfully try to recognise how God is trying to purify you?

7.	Genuine religious experience and divine guidance, usually lead to a greater sense of inner freedom. As St Paul observed: 'Where the Spirit of the Lord is, there is freedom' 2 Corinthians 3: 17. Do you find that instead of living your life on the basis of cheerless duty, you are increasingly motivated by a joyful sense of inner conviction?

8.	St Paul asked rhetorically in 2 Corinthians 13: 5 'Do you not realise that Jesus Christ is within you?'

Besides being aware of the transcendence of the loving God beyond you, are you also aware of the immanence of Christ's loving presence within, enabling you, by the power of the Holy Spirit, to live in Him all that he himself lived?

9.   When you are conscious of the love of God, do you try to see and love in others, especially the poor and the oppressed, what the Lord is seeing and loving in you? Does your love find practical expression in deeds of mercy and action for justice: in other words, is your hand conformed to your heart?

10.   Those who have a spiritual outlook appreciate the fact that the existence of the world around them, the countless blessings they have received, are all the gifts of God.   Not only that, they believe that evil, their own and that of others, never has the last word. It belongs to God and it is always a word of blessing. Do you express gratitude always and for everything (Cf. 1 Thessalonians 5: 17-18), by thanking and praising God in all circumstances, good and bad alike?

Diagnosis Leads to Remedial Action

When you have done your best to answer the ten questions, you will be more aware of your charismatic state of health. If you got 0–10 you are in an unhealthy state; if you got 11–20 you are moderately healthy; if you got from 21–30 you are enjoying good charismatic health. It is worth noting that, the results are merely intended to be humourously indicative rather than statistically accurate. Just as the doctor would make recommendations on the basis of a physical check-up, so a spiritual director could make recommendations on the basis of a charismatic inventory. I suspect that he or she might encourage you to concentrate on the following three points.

Firstly, spend time in prayer every day. Ask God, not only to fill you with the Holy Spirit, but to help you to acknowledge whatever might be blocking that in-filling. Ask with confidence, mindful of the promise of Jesus: 'If you who are evil, know how to give good gifts to your children, how much more will the heavenly Father give the Holy Spirit to those who ask him!' Luke 11: 13.

Secondly, the charismatic ethic can be summed up in the words of Paul in Gallations 5: 16 'live by the Spirit.' Every day ask the Lord for divine guidance. You can do so by saying a prayer like the following, 'Father in heaven, your Spirit is a Spirit of truth and love. Pour that same Holy Spirit into my body, mind and soul. Preserve me today from all illusion and false inspirations. Reveal your Presence and your purposes to me in a way I can understand. And I thank you that you will do this, while giving me that ability to respond, through Christ our Lord. Amen.'

Thirdly, believe that when God reveals the divine will, you will be empowered to carry it out even to the point of healings and miracles. Before embarking on any task, especially a demanding one, you might say the prayer already mentioned in chapter 4: 'Lord, the good

I wish to do, I cannot do, but you are living out the mysteries of your life in me. Enable me by the Spirit that animated your loving service, to continue and fulfill that same loving service in my own life. Give me the ability to do this task, and I thank you that you will achieve even more than I can ask, or imagine through the power of your Spirit at work within me.'

Conclusion

The check-up proposed here, not only intends to help you to gauge your charismatic state of health, it also aims to help you to identify what you could do to improve it.

*To purchase further copies of this book or
to obtain our catalogue, contact*

Goodnews Books & Audio
15 Barking Close
Luton, Beds
LU4 9HG, UK

*Good Christian Books
Online and by Mail Order*

Tel: 01582 571011
Fax: 01582 571012
orders@goodnewsbooks.net
www.goodnewsbooks.net
(secure on-line shopping)